to Vi—
belated
wishes
of love —
    Marilyn —
      X
2005

THE PRICE OF WATER
IN FINISTÈRE

Bodil Malmsten

THE PRICE OF WATER
IN FINISTÈRE

Translated from the Swedish by
Frank Perry

THE HARVILL PRESS

LONDON

Published by The Harvill Press 2005

2 4 6 8 10 9 7 5 3 1

Originally published with the title *Priset på vatten I Finistère*
by Albert Bonniers Förlag, Stockholm, 2001

First published in Great Britain in 2005 by
The Harvill Press
Random House, 20 Vauxhall Bridge Road,
London SWIV 2SA

Random House Australia (Pty) Limited
20 Alfred Street, Milsons Point, Sydney,
New South Wales 2061, Australia

Random House New Zealand Limited
18 Poland Road, Glenfield,
Auckland 10, New Zealand

Random House South Africa (Pty) Limited
Endulini, 5A Jubilee Road, Parktown 2193, South Africa

The Random House Group Limited Reg. No. 954009
www.randomhouse.co.uk/harvill

A CIP catalogue record for this book is available from the British Library

ISBN 1 84343 164 5

Grateful acknowledgement is made to Weidenfeld & Nicolson for permission
to quote a few lines from *Tulipomania* by Mike Dash

This book has been published with the financial assistance
of the Swedish Institute

Papers used by Random House are natural, recyclable products made from
wood grown in sustainable forests; the manufacturing processes conform
to the environmental regulations of the country of origin

Typeset by SX Composing DTP, Rayleigh, Essex
Printed and bound in Great Britain by
William Clowes Ltd, Beccles, Suffolk

Contents

For my editor, Andrea Belloli

Far Away and All Alone

I'M IN MY GARDEN in Finistère filling out change-of-address cards. It's an afternoon at the beginning of September 2000, a soft haze over the countryside. The Atlantic is breathing tides and seaweed, the reassuring sound of the warning buoy like an owl.

I live in Finistère because I've moved here. It wasn't by chance; for a woman of experience there's no such thing as chance.

Sleep with open eyes and you shall find.

A couple of months, that's all it took. I left the country I'd lived in for fifty-five years, the time had come. Drunk on freedom I drove away; I wasn't looking, but I found Finistère. Not far from Brest I felt I was getting close and then it wasn't long before I was standing in front of the parcel of paradise that is mine.

In the same way that there's a partner for every person, there's a place. All you have to do is find your own among the billions that belong to other people, you have to be awake, you have to choose.

My place lies where the land comes to an end in Europe – *fin des terres, finis terrae* – Finistère.

This landscape is mine, we belong together, the changes

in the weather, the extremes. No rain so unrelenting and suddenly the sun rips the curtains of cloud apart.

The coast is one of the most dangerous in the world, the most dangerous. Cliffs and sandbanks, tidal currents. This is where the oil tanker *Erika* went down during the last winter of the twentieth century, the winter before I arrived. This coast is mine now, my storms.

From the very first storm I knew – this is where I'm going to die but not for a very long time.

The trees, the paths, the fields. Gigantic trees, primeval vegetation. The footpaths run through tunnels and away towards the steep beaches of the bay.

I wasn't washed ashore, I took the decision, fortune favours the prepared.

At first sight I knew – this is for the rest of my life.

Here or nowhere, here or not at all.

I sign the change-of-address cards, put stamps on and air-mail stickers and send them off.

A time of happiness follows, of total well-being, euphoria. I find myself in that blessed state of mind in which everything is possible, everything can be constructed, everything repaired. At this point the garden is nothing but a few hundred square metres of parched lawn, the guest room still only a mildewed corner of the garage. The guest room might turn into an airy loft with its own staircase, the garden might become a leafy paradise.

Not a cloud in the sky. It's dry, so I water.

Then the telephone starts ringing, e-mails arrive and

the letter box on the fence-post overflows. My change-of-address cards have reached their destinations.

Instead of making those close to me happy, I've given them a terrible fright. My city friends sound just as dismayed as Grandma would have done, my maternal grandmother, Karin Olivia Alm, *neé* Jönsson, of the inland areas and mountains of central Norrland. The cowshed's burning, the Russians are coming. What a calamity, mercy me. This is bound to end in tears.

You can't just move that far away all on your own!

Everyone sounds like my Grandma.

In the land where I was born, love is indissolubly linked to terror.

Moving away, so far away. And all alone.

Far away and all alone.

I spend a couple of days trying to calm people down even though I know full well that calm comes from within, never by post.

If there's loneliness here, I brought it with me – Finistère is full of people, there are 838,687 Finistèrians dispersed over appropriate distances. There is no far away anymore, if ever there was. Where you are is where the centre is.

Even if we're heading for the Stone Age, the Earth is still round.

There's nothing new under the sun, Grandma's in heaven and I'm in Finistère.

Woe is me.

The cowshed's burning in Brittany and the Russians are coming for the Chechens.

It is bound to end in tears.

It always has and it always will as long as Man disposes and the god Grandma believed in looks the other way.

Things are the way they are.

I'm not on my own, I'm the 838,688th Finistèrian.

I once was lost but now I am found.

All is calm.

The reason I left was that I didn't know where to turn any more, I was completely lost in the land of my fathers, I had to leave, but I had no idea where to go.

I didn't know Finistère existed. All I knew was that I couldn't stay or I would die and I didn't want that.

It's easy when you know how. I had no choice.

I set off on a Sunday, April 16, 2000. Overcast, light traffic. The car packed, the flat sold, the furniture given away.

No goodbyes. The people I love I carry within me, no farewells. A brief glance in the rear-view mirror. Goodbye Formica Housing Coop, we'll never meet again.

I knew what I was leaving but not where I was going.

I took the E4, the trans-European motorway south-bound, not northbound.

There are no trans-European motorways that lead to the inland areas and mountains of central Norrland where I grew up. What roads there are up there are mostly pot-holes, and they all lead to Stockholm.

No matter how many call-centres are established in isolated villages.

I took the train to Stockholm, where I got stuck, and spent a lifetime there until I left.

It's easy when you know how. I had no alternative.

"If only we could," they all said, when I told them I was leaving. People I knew and didn't know, my neighbours, the post-office staff whom I told I was moving. A taxi driver from Tunisia called Amor, they all said it.

"If only we could, if it wasn't for the kids, work, the language. If only I could get away from here, I'd just take the family and go."

I did it.

It's easy if you know how.

I knew how because I have everything you need to leave. I have everything except a country of my own to come back to. My Granddad built it up, and it doesn't exist any more.

Building up, tearing down. That's the way of the world. Too bad, but not something to obsess about at 180 kilometres an hour on the *Autobahn*.

I'm leaving the old behind, but I'm taking history with me. How could it be otherwise?

A person without history or roots is a shell. Take history away and the only thing left on the *Autobahn* will be the cars, I'm driving on the history of Europe, a motorway of blood, an artery of evil.

The fact that, unlike the welfare state my Granddad helped construct, the *Autobahn* hasn't been demolished has to do with the human capacity for repression, that talent people have for looking the other way when it suits them, for pretending not to see. If the capacity for repression didn't exist, the entire human race would have been wiped out, there wouldn't be six billion human beings on earth, but six at most, two of whom would be George Bush.

I'm glad the *Autobahn* exists. That I've got a car, that I'm allowed to drive this Rover as fast as it can go and poison Europe the way it's poisoning me, I'm wild with freedom and insanely happy.

I'm driving away from the old on the old at two hundred kilometres an hour. No-one knows I'm on my way to Finistère, no-one knows anything. You might die at any moment – that's the way it is.

I want to sing a hymn to what has been and what will be and what is, I'm intoxicated with speed and exhilarated. I want to sing a hymn, so I do.

On the road to Maastricht, I sing number 521 from the hymn-book as we sang it in the village school every new morning:

> Morning on the mountains
> Hark in field and wood
> To the streams and fountains
> Singing: God is good

God isn't good because he doesn't exist. I'm not good because it's not possible; I'm a human being and I exist. Happy and free, even if it's not possible.

Nothing is past, everything happens again and simultaneously.

The world never learns, it begins again.

The worst has already happened and won't ever stop happening. The great wound bleeds; it has no edge, no boundary. No-one can ignore it. That's the way it is. People know, but they have to go on living. Powerless and fragile, human beings aren't free, they're imprisoned and under threat. Being unhappy is useless, you have to be happy, being happy is an obligation and a responsibility.

The world is full of tears. Someone has to cry them, and so I do at two hundred kilometres an hour until the *Autobahn* comes to an end.

Nie wieder, Autobahn. Auf wiedersehen.

I switch on the windscreen-wipers.

An overpass spans Normandy like a rainbow, I stop at its foot, drink coffee and smoke in a lay-by. The landscape is vast like the inland areas and mountains of central Norrland, only with the sea on the horizon instead of mountains.

The lay-by sits on a rise covered in primroses, I pick a huge bunch. My entire childhood in the scent of bright yellow primroses with very green leaves.

My sister and I on our red bikes on our way to the primrose hill. Just a moment ago it was 35° below zero. Now the snow has melted, we race our bikes to the primrose hill. There's barely any time to gather the precious primroses after the winter.

We must do it.

Why else would the entire hillside be covered in primroses? As quick to vanish as the coltsfoot on the railway embankment, the blue anemones along the edges of the forest, the catkins on the willow twigs. To be savoured, one by one. The bikes hurled by the roadside because we must pick the primroses before the frost comes.

How else would there be time for the lilies-of-the-valley?

We gather primroses in bunches so big our hands won't reach round them.

I get my hands from Grandma.

"Mercy me," Grandma said, "poor child. Having to put up with hands as big as mine, just like a man's. Mercy me."

One of her Mercy me's didn't come true, I didn't grow to be as tall as her, as tall as a bean-pole. When I turned eleven, I put a stop to growing to make Grandma happy. Happiness wasn't in her repertoire. The flow of Mercy me's was constant. The freckles. The red hair. I was the recipient of her endless worry.

The cowshed's burning, we'll soon be in the workhouse.

The Russians are coming. Mercy me.

I leave behind the primrose mound in Normandy, the Normandy of the landings, the beautiful Picardy of the song: "Roses are blooming in Picardy." And by the evening of the third day I'm in Finistère, and here I have been for a year and more, this precious year.

I live here now and it's incredible, inexpressible and indescribable.

There are no words.

So what do I do but go and promise Madame C I'll write about it.

I say to Madame C: It's so wonderful here that one should write a book about it.

"One should write a book about it," I say.

"So do it!" says Madame C.

Woe is me.

Once upon a Time in Paradise

It's so wonderful here that one should write a book about it, people say.

Without meaning anything more than that it's wonderful in Finistère.

Someone ought to write a book about it.

It's the kind of thing you say when the mimosa's in bloom and a *Magnolia stellata* bursts into flower, white stars on a bare branch.

A writer shouldn't be so careless with words, but I'm only a writer when I write.

It's a sunny morning in the middle of September, my first September in Finistère, it happens to be my birthday. I'm walking round the garden wishing myself many happy returns. My very first garden, I can do whatever I want. There is no-one to say "What do you think you're up to?" or "Now look what you've gone and done!"

No advice, no instructions.

I'm relying on my intuition and my memory. Trying to remember the way the plants were set out in Grandmother's garden, my paternal grandmother's garden outside Stockholm, and what Grandma's was like up in the north.

Grandmother's peonies flowered in the meadow where they had plenty of sun, although in the course of the day the shade from the balsam poplars in the drive would wander across them.

The soil in Grandma's flowerbeds was chalky and cold. Tiger lilies, iris and columbines flowered against the south-facing wall. It was sunny and sheltered from the wind.

Grandmother had an arch of white roses by the steps up from the meadow.

Grandma had monkshood by the root cellar.

Grandmother had raspberry canes and Grandma gooseberry bushes, but ever since my younger sister and I ate ourselves sick on unripe gooseberries I've lost any appetite for berries. Our intestines were in knots. We were sent to the hospital in an ambulance and had to lie on the ward with little tubes in our bottoms to stop us dying.

No berry bushes.

The part of the garden that borders the neighbour's is going to be a white garden inspired by Vita Sackville-West's white garden at Sissinghurst. The names they have!

Gertrude Jekyll was another famous British gardening lady; whether or not she turned into Gertrude Hyde at night and planted black flowers is something they fail to mention in my British gardening book.

I've got three gardening books. An English one, a French one, a Swedish one, and none of them are any use. The Swedish one is full of sentimental twaddle, flowers "open their little blue eyes", "stand on transparent legs", "have dashing moustaches", "curl up with distaste".

The French one is in French and the British one is preposterous.

According to the English gardening book, it takes an entire lifetime to get a garden to look natural. Provided you do nothing else. To get a garden to look wild, everything must be planned down to the last blade of grass. Before you can so much as contemplate sowing a single seed, you have to ascertain the precise angle of the sun at various times of day and how the shadows from the trees and house fall in the morning, afternoon and evening. You have to draw up a sunlight chart and arrange your garden accordingly.

I'm not the kind of person who draws up sunlight charts. Unless it's your natural inclination, you should refrain from any attempt to draw up a sunlight chart. Otherwise you'll end up with hell instead of the paradise you wanted.

In my white garden, white hollyhocks, white mallows, white carnations, white poppies and white hellebores will bloom.

White narcissi — *Narcissus poeticus*, the poet's narcissus — white pearl hyacinths, huge white hyacinths.

White lily-flowering tulips, white lilies.

At the back I'll have sweet peas in various colours, dark blue, red and pink, flaming yellow nasturtiums and a sky-blue vine with bell-shaped flowers called *Cobaea*.

Blue lobelia will tumble down the gate-posts like water-falls. A green wire fence surrounds the property, it will be covered in sweet peas. A screen of scented sweet peas will protect the garden against anyone looking in until the hedges have grown up; laurel hedges or a rose hedge remains to be seen.

Laurels grow more quickly, but a rose hedge is a rose hedge is a rose hedge . . .

There will be red flowers facing the village road. A scarlet sweet pea will glow against the glossy green leaves of a thicket of pittosporum. The translucent swirls of the sweet pea will contrast with the glabrous oblong dark green pittosporum leaves.

When the sweet pea finishes flowering, it will be succeeded by very dark red sunflowers. The sunflowers shoot up to over two metres and are easy to grow. "A flower that is easy to grow and popular with children" it says on the seed-packet. If the sweet pea is still in flower when the sunflowers appear, it will climb up their thick stems.

Plants are going to climb and ramble all over my garden, jungle-like and apparently wild.

Since I've never had a garden before, the first year will be for experimenting. Better too much than too little. Too much is never enough, too much is nothing, you never know what's going to come up.

What came up and what froze in the inland areas and mountains of central Norrland was a matter of divine providence, Grandma used to say.

Most things froze apart from the wild chervil and cat's-foot; what did come up was nurtured with extraordinary devotion. The flowers that were cherished the most were orchids.

The fact that orchids thrive in that cold chalk soil is a

source of perennial pride up there. Ceremonial visits were paid to these wild and protected deities, so worshipped and adored. The tiny chocolate-coloured, chocolate-scented Black Vanilla orchid by the cold spring above Grandma's house, the Lady's Slipper beside the forest tarns.

Thousands of different orchids flowered in roadside ditches, each more remarkable, and more protected, than the next. The common spotted orchid, pyramidal saxifrage, the fragrant orchid and wood cow-wheat, that's how it was when I was a child. Then they started spraying with DDT, and now they've got the National Roads Agency threatening to scrape the orchids away.

Last I heard, some of my relatives were trying to protect the orchids by forming a human shield against the road-graders.

Just as I'm feeling the depth of the soil by the fence along the village road — it's on the shallow side — a small purple Peugeot stops by my gate.

A woman my own age opens the car door as though it were a theatre curtain. What emerges is the vision that will turn out to be Madame C. All the light gathers on her figure. Never have I seen anyone carry their body and their clothes with such elegance, like a gift to the world, a present. Her make-up is a work of art with the hallmark of a masterpiece: the beauty is apparent but not the effort. Gracefully she places a pair of strappy sandals firmly on the gravel and walks lightly on her long legs up to my gate calling "*Bonjour, Madame.*"

Reluctantly I pull my hand out of the soil and go over to the fence. What could this flamboyant creature want that's important enough to take me away from my soil?

She just wants to let me know she exists, she says. Extending a lovely manicured hand on which a wire-thin diamond ring glitters, she introduces herself as Madame C.

I wipe the soil off my own hand on my trouser leg, hold it out and mumble my peculiar name, where I come from and that I live here now.

"I know," Madame C says with a dazzling smile and a handshake that belies her delicate slimness.

Then she says, "Enjoy the rest of the afternoon," walks back to her car, gathers up her dress and gets into her purple Peugeot, her strappy sandals the last to disappear. A glimpse of scarlet nail varnish on her toes and she is gone.

I stand there like a subterranean animal, a mole, blinking in the light.

The car vanishes in the direction of the harbour while a distinct fragrance of sweet peas lingers.

From that day on, Madame C will stop at my fence on her way to buy her daily baguette or shellfish in the harbour with its twelve different kinds of oysters. As time passes I'll make the same kind of visits to Madame C's gate.

We'll exchange a few words. At the beginning I've nothing to contribute, but Madame C will share her abundance.

I'll come to be very fond of the way she always provides

synonyms for the words I am looking for. Of never being satisfied with the first word – *le mot, la parole.*

When we disagree, which we often will do, Madame C will supply me with the words I need to contradict her – *porter la contradiction dans le débat.*

We'll talk about the weather and the best way of killing little creatures. About Jacques Chirac, about Commander Massoud, the Afghan resistance hero who makes both our hearts beat faster. About literature, about the importance of being alive. We'll talk about death and ageing, we'll exchange views about everything that grows.

About the book, the bloody book that hasn't even been thought of yet – not thought of by Madame C, not promised by me.

That first meeting so crucial to every relationship has occurred. The rules have been established, the roles assigned.

If we were going to be lovers, it would already be obvious which one of us would make the beds and who would wash the car – me.

But there is as little likelihood of Madame C and me becoming lovers as there is of Monsieur Le R, my ex-*Rosenkavalier* Monsieur Le R, and me.

No love stories.

Not with people, it's too difficult. I'm still in love's kindergarten and all I'm really ready for is a bit of soil and a spade. For now.

From September 15 to that fateful day in February, when I promise Madame C to write a book about my Finistère, I am completely happy, completely free. A calm flow of days, one after another, I walk around my garden being happy.

Half a year in paradise – that would be as much as anyone gets.

Stone Sale

"Good luck," the neighbours say when they see me working in the garden. "*Bon courage, Madame*."

I'm preparing the ground to lay a stone path across the garden, based on a picture in *Le Jardin* and using as my model one of the perfect stone paths my ex-*Rosenkavalier*, Monsieur Le R, had in his perfect garden.

"*Bon courage*," the neighbours say. "Good courage with the digging, Madame."

That is the way they put things in Finistère. If it's at the beginning of the afternoon, they greet you with "Good beginning to the afternoon," if it's at the end of the afternoon, "Good end to the afternoon."

Every part of the day, every task, has its own blessing.

Bonne après-midi, bon matin. Good forenoon, good afternoon, good evening, good courage. Good planting, good walking.

If I'm painting my garden shed, the children call out, "Good garden-shed painting, Madame." If I'm spraying my "Ingrid Bergman", the modern hybrid rose I've placed next to the entrance facing the village road, my neighbour may very well say, "Good bug-spraying, Madame." His Finistère dialect is as difficult for me to understand as the language in the village where I grew up was incomprehensible to anyone not from there.

When the dentist, the delightful dentist, tells me that my next appointment may have to be cancelled because his wife is due to give birth at about that time, I try to make a joke. This is the first joke I've made that has been understood. "Good childbearing," I say, and the dentist laughs. And not only because he's so nice.

"Good digging," the neighbours shout when they see me working on my stone path. Sometimes they stop to compliment me on my industriousness.

After watering, digging is the kind of gardening work I love most. Sinking the spade's steel blade into the ground, shovelling soil, feeling the spade strike a stone. Getting a grip on the stone, feeling how it can be worked loose. Being able to move stone is a talent I get from my mother, I've got stone-shifting in my blood.

Around the farm in the inland areas and mountains of central Norrland, my mother built a wall with stones she had dug up herself. A wall like the Great Wall of China she built with her own hands. It's only now that I'm capable of appreciating that wall, and that she didn't do it out of martyrdom but with that deep feeling for stone I've inherited from her.

I lay out my stone path. I've dragged the paving-stones into place with the wheelbarrow. These are large paving-stones, half a metre square, five centimetres thick and very heavy. On special offer. The builders' merchants I am a regular at, and where I have a *carte de fidelité*, were having a sale on stone.

I must have made several hundred francs buying the

paving-stones. My father would have recognised my feeling of satisfaction at getting such a bargain.

Being unable to resist a special offer is something I get from my father. My hands come from Grandma and my impulsive, repressive nature from my mother.

When I was young no-one believed that genes had a part to play in who you were. As far as my generation was concerned, environment was the only factor with a decisive role in shaping human life. I still find it difficult to believe that there can be any other form of heredity than the social one, even though I'm proved wrong every time I see my mother.

For plants, the first fifteen days are crucial, for a human being you have to reach much further back, generation upon generation. A human being is more than soil and water and a bit of sunlight.

I never got the chance to talk about this special-offer business with my father, he died before we had the chance to talk about anything, death the all-depriving.

My father is the only one who would understand the pleasure I took in lifting the paving-stones into and out of the car, why I bought thirty boxes of cement tiles, because the price had been reduced from three hundred francs to thirty per box. All the china on special offer, all the plants. This satisfaction at earning by buying, at cheating consumer society, at buying expensive things at reduced prices, it's not a bargain unless the goods are top quality. It's not like archaeological excavations where the least bit of rubbish is a find simply because it's old, my father was an agronomist, not an archaeologist.

To say he could return from a sale of porcelain sanitary ware with ten bidets would be an exaggeration, but not really. The more you buy the more you earn. This was something my father understood and so do I. Shopping at sales is an investment, the kind of investment he believed in even though he was a Communist.

Those tartan woollen dressing-gowns from Härnösand. Indestructible, ankle-length, fitted with a belt at the waist and with pockets stitched on.

Never have so many people received so many tartan woollen dressing-gowns as Christmas presents. Never has a tartan woollen dressing-gown scratched someone's skin as long as the one I still have hanging in the little bedroom in the cottage where I was born. At least fifty years old, but good as new. A full-length tartan woollen dressing-gown like that is what my father thought of as a real bargain.

Even if I'm the only one who can think of anything now.

In Vietnam, people believe the dead go on living in another dimension where they experience the same needs as the living but don't have to deal with the problems the living encounter. In the temples there are altars where gifts to the dead are burned.

A rich Vietnamese might burn a car to his father. This is how the car is transported to the dimension in which his father exists.

If I were Vietnamese I would burn stones to my father.

Making a path with paving-stones is a lot more demanding than you might think just from looking at any ordinary paved garden path.

First the paving-stones have to be laid out according to your length of stride. Then comes the experimental walking, the moving, the levelling.

Having to think about the length of your strides makes walking unnatural. I find myself either falling over or walking with bent knees, whipping my feet in front of me, just like in the *Monty Python* silly walks sketch. As soon as you try to do something naturally, it becomes unnatural, whether it's laying a stone path or writing a book.

You have to try and get back to the way you did it before you became self-conscious, even if you could neither write nor walk then.

When your stride pattern has more or less been dealt with, a shape is chopped out around the edges of the stone and then the stone is lifted away. The space marked out is excavated, the cavity filled with sand. Only then can the paving-stone be put in its final position. A few clumps of grass between the stones and there is your paved path. Adapted to your stride pattern, wonderfully smooth and tranquil.

The thing is that once a paving-stone has been laid, the one preceding it or the one after turns out to be too high or too low. The paving-stones are not level, they slope in various directions.

The only thing to do is begin again, lift off the paving-stone, dig out the ground, pour in more sand or take some away, lay the paving-stone back in place and walk on it once more to test it.

"*Bon courage* with the paving," the neighbours shout.

There's no "*Bon courage* with the paving" from Madame C,

she completely ignores my not easily ignored hard labour – no-one can ignore like Madame C, she thinks I should devote myself to my own profession. Madame C has got it into her head that my imagination needs to be put to use and that my talent for laying stone paving is of no consequence whatever. She turns out to be right.

My paved path will not be perfect and harmonious like the ones in the pictures in the gardening magazines, nor like the path in the garden of Monsieur Le R, my ex-*Rosenkavalier*.

It will be the way it is and that's the way it will be as long as I live.

All the same, had it not been for the neighbours and their "*Bon courage, Madame*" and "Keep up the good work on laying the paving-stones" I would never have managed the preposterous business of laying as many paving-stones as I have.

No Backs

Not to mention all those decisions and resolutions that come to nothing.

You're only human, after all. As an excuse for not fulfilling promises to yourself this is pretty pathetic. Makes it sound like being human means not fulfilling the promises you make to yourself.

One day, on *France Culture*, one of the participants in a cultural debate said: "Animals don't listen to *France Culture*."

I didn't understand whether this was an argument in favour of or against, but it's a good one. Animals don't take part in cultural debates.

Animals don't make resolutions that come to nothing.

No backs was my first resolution when I started work on the garden.

Absolutely no back parts. Since the garden's so small, I'm determined that each and every square centimetre will be the front. There will be nowhere things get shoved aside. Rubbish will immediately be burnt or composted, although since my first composting defeat, I haven't managed to get a new compost heap started. My first compost heap ended up as an enormous slimy fungus behind the garden shed.

Behind, at the back of.

What right do I have to keep setting up hierarchies? What

is there to say that the side with the door in is the front and the one without, the back?

One long side of the garden shed overlooks a vacant piece of land. This side is covered in uprooted weeds, orange peel, two dead mimosa trees, one rubber boot, some cardboard boxes, a plastic bucket with holes in and the firewood for next winter. Rubbish, rubbish, rubbish.

It does nobody any harm since the property on the other side of the fence hasn't been developed and is screened off by hedges and trees. The fact that I've created a back there harms no-one. Except me.

What a bad thing it is to say no-one is harmed by it when I am! It's like saying no-one's home when you're there. Or no-one's going to notice when the bed's left unmade, the washing-up's not been done and you've let yourself go.

This annihilation of self, the lethal negation of your own existence.

I am made to suffer by the back I've created and so it has to go. I'm exposing myself to suffering, to a lack of respect. The only thing to do is to remake the back as the front, the only thing to do is begin again.

Man is put on Earth to begin again, beginning again is what it means to be a human being, being no-one is something only the dead can indulge in.

No backs.

The Little Oaks

Acorns drop from the neighbour's oak trees over the fence and onto my drive. One day, a week or so after I move in, the woman next door asks if I mind the acorns dropping over the fence.

No, I don't. On the contrary.

"*Tant pis,*" I say, smiling, and she smiles back.

I only discover that *tant pis* doesn't mean "on the contrary" a lot later when looking up the word *mole* — *taupe* ~ *f* — and my gaze happens to fall on *tant pis* ~ *too bad*.

It's not too bad that acorns drop into my garden, it's a blessing, I love trees and everything about them.

There are two ash trees in my garden, enormous old trees with great crowns and palmate leaves. Those wonderful tree-tops are full of dead branches, there's a profusion of vole holes around the roots, the trunks are suffocating because of all the lichen that covers them, and I don't dare scrape it away for fear of damaging the trees. I don't dare spray them either, I'm afraid my ash trees are going to die.

There's a tree expert in Quimperlé, Monsieur Godot the arboriculturist, only he's very expensive, according to Madame C. And anyway, he never turns up, but that's the way things are. According to Madame C.

One rainy day in October I discover that an acorn has taken root. Two tiny oak leaves are shooting up out of a puddle. If I hadn't happened to catch sight of them, I would have crushed them underfoot. When I look at them more closely, I notice that the oak leaves are sitting on top of a stem as thin as sewing-thread but standing upright all the same. A little rope trick in the rain. The fact that this miniature can turn into an oak tree is one of the miracles of nature you have to see to believe.

I decide to give the miracle a helping hand, and so begins my cultivation of oak trees.

First I build a barricade against the sea winds, a wall of little stones around the shoot. Then a bamboo stick as support and warning. Finally, a sawn-off mineral-water bottle as a greenhouse over the diminutive oak tree and as protection against the storms I've been warned about.

From the moment the growing period starts once winter's over, I feed the oak shoot small quantities of peat every other week.

When I measure it in the middle of the growing season, my oak has reached a height of 12 centimetres — 120 millimetres. If the stem is stretched to its full extent, this becomes 132.

I give it fertiliser.

In the inland areas and mountains of central Norrland, it's almost all spruce. Pines and fir trees. Quivering aspens. We had rowans in our garden, but rowans don't live to be old, they wither and die before long. Grandma had a maple outside her kitchen window. No oaks.

There are no oak trees where I grew up. My sister and I

were the only children in the village who'd ever seen an oak. This was because our father came from Stockholm, a cause for shame as well as pride. It made no difference that we'd been born in the village, my sister and I were outcasts.

Our father was upper class. Not just in relation to the villagers because of his coming from Stockholm, he was upper class in relation to most people in Stockholm. He grew up in a manor house surrounded by ancient oaks under which he and his brothers played.

Where my sister and I grew up, children played with the cones from fir and pine trees. All those rickety fir-cone cows and pine-cone sheep with matchstick legs that were never the same length, all those fir-cone pens and pine-cone fences.

My father and his brothers made soldiers out of their acorns. Without being aware of it, they'd already begun to arm themselves for the rebellion that children of the urban upper classes were destined to make in those days.

In the '30s my father and his brothers joined Clarté, "an international socialist organisation, made up largely of intellectuals, founded by Henri Barbusse in 1919", as it says in the concise Swedish encyclopaedia I use.

My not using the fourteen-volume reference work left me by my father is partly to do with it being out of date – a lot of phrenology and savages wearing penis-sheaths – and partly because I left it behind in the village.

The fact that my little encyclopaedia is not called *kompakt* but "compact" reflects the fact that it was published in Sweden in the late 1990s. Instead of becoming the dictatorship of the proletariat my father and his upper-class comrades dreamt of, Sweden has become a vassal state of the US.

Shit or *fucking shit* are the commonest swearwords in my homeland nowadays.

My father never swore. If he needed to say "shit" he said "sugar".

He often did.

No-one could get as angry as my father, it's from him I get the rage I don't know how to cope with.

Once he got so angry that he clipped me round the ear. We were camping on the island of Gotland, my father, my sister and I. It was my turn to light the Primus stove and I was scared.

"I can't," I said.

"There is no such word as *can't*," he said, and swish! his hand lashed out before he could stop it. Bang and his palm was against my cheek.

He was as shocked as I was. Since no matter how much rage he had, that was the only slap he ever gave me. Neither he nor I would have believed that it was a gift that still comes in handy today, but that is the case.

Every time I'm about to say, or ever have said, "I can't," I feel that swish.

There's no such thing as *can't*, bang.

In my homeland there's a saying: Spare the rod, spoil the child. Neither my father nor I would ever have subscribed to such idiocy. Deliberately hurting the person you love, what hideous perversion! And yet I got more out of that slap than from all my father's well-meaning advice about how to live your life as a good socialist.

Such an infinity of things we never had time to discuss because death adjourned the debate. Violence and non-violence, Stalin and the gulag, China, freedom of expression in Vietnam. The former Yugoslavia – Milosevic! Hungary, Lech Walesa, Solidarity.

Sweden!

If my father were alive today, he'd be so enraged that it would kill him. If he wasn't enraged, it'd be even worse. It's best that he's dead.

Only it isn't. Death is the worst thing that can come between people, I want to show him my oak saplings, I want to talk about Afghanistan, about Iraq, Daddy.

I want to give you a book that crosses party lines. I want to talk to you about *The Man Who Planted Trees* by Jean Giono.

The man who plants trees in the book is called Elzéard Bouffier.

Elzéard Bouffier lives on a farm in the French alpilles with his sheep and his sheepdog. His wife and his only son are dead, he is, as they say, alone in the world. Despite the fact that the world is full of people of every kind and denomination, that's what people say when someone's family and friends aren't there in the flesh.

While Elzéard Bouffier watches over his sheep, he realises that there are too few trees. This is killing the land. The ground is as hard as rock. There's no water. The poor peasants trying to make a living are completely at the mercy of the wind and the weather. People are giving up.

Elzéard Bouffier makes up his mind to put things right and starts planting trees. He begins at the turn of the century and continues until he dies in 1947. He goes on planting through two world wars, tirelessly, day after day. He keeps on planting from Verdun to Hiroshima. He covers an entire hillside in his part of the Vaucluse with verdant oak woods. Springs well up, people who had to move away from the impoverished villages return, schools reopen.

A single man who decides to devote his life to planting trees. Mostly oaks.

During the autumn I discover some more oak shoots, which I nurture as carefully as the first one. On my morning and evening rounds, I examine my tiny oak trees. If they are wilting, I feed them; if pests attack, I spray them. If there's a drought, I water them.

Even if not all the oak saplings survive, some will. Oak trees are hardy and grow easily in Finistère.

Thanks to my neighbour's acorns, I'll have a stand of oak trees here in ten years. In twenty years, a grove; in twenty-five, an oak wood will provide shade and moisture for this part of the garden. A spring could well up. Wild boar will root for truffles where now there's only gravel.

In twenty-five years I'll only be eighty with many years left to enjoy my garden.

I need the oaks to replace the ash trees when they're gone for good.

It's doubtful whether even the expensive arboriculturist from Quimperlé could save the ash trees. It may be that their time is over. In *Facts about Trees* by J. Bretaudeau, there's no information about the life expectancy of the common ash – *Fraxinus excelsior*.

What is emphasised is that the male tree grows faster

than the female, and taller, up to 40 metres in height, but it says nothing about whether the male also dies earlier and at what age.

I'm just about to climb up into the ash trees to saw off the withered branches in their crowns when I realise that I'll soon be fifty-six years old.

I nurse the little oaks as though they were my children.

A garden without trees isn't a garden.

I water my oak shoots so as not to die.

The Man Who Planted Trees is one of the stories in a series *Reader's Digest* put together in the '50s. A number of authors were asked to write about the most remarkable person they had ever met. Jean Giono was invited to take part and wrote the story about Elzéard Bouffier in a few days and sent it in. The editors of *Reader's Digest* responded by return of post. *The Man Who Planted Trees* was exactly the sort of story they were looking for.

A week later and Giono receives a letter in which the shocked editors accuse him of being a fraudster, a charlatan, a distorter of facts. It has come to their attention that the man who planted trees didn't exist. Elzéard Bouffier was no mortal man of woman born but a fictional creation. The wonderful oak woods described in the book grew out of Giono's imagination. If there are oak trees in the Vaucluse, it wasn't Elzéard Bouffier who planted them, and he didn't pass quietly away in the hospital in Banon in 1947.

The editors are furious.

Jean Giono finds their reaction insane. To ask an author, a professional writer, to write about the most remarkable person he has met and then be shocked that this person is fictional!

What shocks me is that Jean Giono wrote the story in a few days. It says so on the back of the book, in passing, not to show off. "A few days later he delivered the typescript of the story."

If I were to write a story about the most remarkable person I've ever met it would take the rest of my life to make up my mind whether or not it is Madame C, only I'm not going to.

I walk round my garden, feeding my little oak trees while talking gardening and politics with my father.

The Peonies

The peonies are here. Scented French peonies, white ones, "Le Cygne" – the swan. Next year, or the year after, "Le Cygne" will be flowering in my garden. Long after I'm dead they'll still be here with their many-layered white flowers whose petals have red streaks running along them like nerves.

Grandmother had peonies in her lovely garden. Pale pink scented double peonies whose name I don't know.

When the pink peonies came into flower in the manor garden, Grandmother would snip them, wearing the cotton dresses her seamstress ran up for her, with a basket on one arm and a pair of secateurs. Only Grandmother was allowed to do the snipping. *Snipping* was one of Grandmother's words. The snipping done, she'd fill the vases in the library, the dining room and the large reception room with gorgeously scented pale pink peonies. Nowhere did the peonies show themselves to better advantage than in Grandmother's blue and white Chinese vases made of porcelain as thin as the peonies' petals and as transparent.

Grandmother taught me how to pick peonies.

A peony should be picked as soon as the little bud shows the colour of its petals, then it will flower in the vase and last longer.

"Little bud" was one of Grandmother's phrases.

You weren't supposed to take the whole stem; a few leaves had to be left so that the peony would flower as profusely the following year. And the year after that.

Grandmother's peonies were older than she was. The peonies were already there when she arrived as a young bride. When she taught me how to pick peonies, a long time had passed since then, a lot of blood had flowed. A child always knows when there's a war in the family, the child has to choose sides and gets torn in two.

When I walked in the scent of the peonies with Grandmother, I was on Grandmother's side, when she referred to the peony bud as the little bud, I said "little bud".

When I sat in Grandma's farm kitchen and smelt the lilacs she brought indoors to stand in a jug on the oilcloth, it was Grandma's side I was on.

It was Grandma I resembled, to Grandmother I bore no resemblance.

"And thus the heart's halves are torn in two," says the god Indra's daughter in Strindberg's *A Dream Play*.

Strindberg does not mention the fact that human beings aren't doomed to reach the end of their days with hearts torn in two, that a garden can put the two halves together again.

I'll have both lilacs and peonies in my garden. My heritage from Grandmother and my heritage from Grandma will be combined without discord.

Strindberg is a very Swedish writer, a genius at describing an inferno and not a single tip about how to escape. Nevertheless, he spent long periods outside Sweden and wrote *A Madman's Defence* in French, *Le Plaidoyer d'un fou*, a prodigious and admirable accomplishment.

Whether the lilacs and the peonies will flower at the same time in Finistère or whether the peonies will come after the lilacs will only become clear in a few years' time. The peonies will probably flower last. Making everyone wait, like royalty at a premiere. The later in the day, the posher the people.

Peonies are named for Paion, doctor to the gods.

If lilacs have anything to do with higher beings, it would be with the pixies who lived in the shadows during winter in the village. Grandma had seen one of these sprites, he'd been grey and had disappeared with an ugly grin behind the big barn.

I buy my "Le Cygne" at a garden centre on the road to Lorient. Not at the rose nursery where I met Monsieur Le R but not far away.

The garden centre where I buy the peonies is a very expensive nursery where they charge absurd amounts of money for plants compared with the one I'm a regular at. The only reason I ever go to the expensive place is to compare prices and work out how much I earn by not shopping there.

These profit margins on which I survive.

All the same, I have to buy the peony plants there. If you ever get the chance to acquire "Le Cygne" you have to take it, cost what it may. Feeling guilty at betraying my usual garden centre and for squandering so much money, I buy three peonies and carry them out to the car. I place them carefully on the passenger seat. Having fastened my seatbelt, I'm about to fasten one around the plants as well, but it's not quite long enough.

Once home I reverently unwrap the packages. The peony plants are nothing more than a few dry leaves on sticks. They're supposed to be like that. Once planted in their holes they'll turn out as magnificently as my Grandmother's peonies did. I hope.

The peony is a demanding plant, I had no idea just how demanding until I read about peonies in the gardening books.

The fact that a flower as gentle and delightful as the peony should be so exacting and dictate such harsh terms hits me with the force of a cold shower. It's just like my girlfriends when I was a teenager, it was always the loveliest and most yielding ones who ran everything. Madame C also comes to mind, Madame C whose gentle manner conceals a strength without limit.

According to the English gardening book, peonies are so fussy that you might as well not bother. You'd need to go back generations to discover the composition of the soil, you'd have to go right back to the Big Bang to find out how the elements are distributed in your garden. You'd have to use the sunlight chart I repudiated to determine the availability of the dappled shade so vital to the peony. You'd also have to know the precise acidity of the soil and in which parts of the garden it is chalk and in which clay. The English gardening book is preposterous, the French one is in French, my "Le Cygne" cuttings will be planted in accord with the Swedish gardening book.

Madame C will not be asked.

The French word for peony is *pivoine*. Pride prevents me from standing there saying *piovine*, or *pivione*.

When it comes to peony planting, the Swedish gardening book is a veritable orgy of qualities characteristic of the land of the Middle Way.

"Peonies require the appropriate amount of fertiliser at the time of planting," it says. "Not too much, not too little." If you happen to give them too little, you can always add more afterwards, but giving them too much isn't a good idea. Then again this needn't be entirely disastrous – there's always an escape clause! The soil shouldn't be too deficient in chalk, although soil with too high a chalk content isn't recommended.

There's always some way or other of ensuring that the amount is not too much and not too little.

Against my natural inclination, I plant the peonies according to these instructions. It's only when I get to the earth-mounds that the whole process comes to a stop.

"Cover the peonies with an earth-mound in the first few years."

An earth-mound!

That's gardening books for you. They always take for granted that you know the very things you bought the gardening book to find out. When I look up earth-mounds in the index, there's no explanation of what one is or how to make it. Is heaping earth around the peonies all it means, or is an earth-mound something you can buy in a garden shop?

In the index there's a gaping hole between "dwarf

37

varieties" and "earthworm" where "earth-mound" should be.

While I'm skimming through the index I might as well look up moles. In the Swedish gardening book moles are found together with hedgehogs and bats under the heading "Other friendly small animals". "They do no great harm," it says. I close the index of the Swedish gardening book for the very last time.

There's no help to be got there, it's between me and the moles now. Like Monsieur Le R in his geometric garden, I have come to learn what vermin moles are. It goes without saying that the Swedish gardening book refuses to acknowledge a fact of this kind.

When it comes to the practicalities of war, my homeland remains, as ever, neutral.

The Promise

A silent drizzle is falling one mild afternoon in February, I'm kneeling by the fence along the village road planting sweet-pea seeds.

I've lived here for six months now, six months in heaven.

It's raining softly. A faint breeze off the sea.

I score grooves in the soil with a fork, make holes and poke in the sweet-pea seeds with a teaspoon. Two to three sweet-pea seeds in each hole, then the seeds have to be covered over. I mix fertiliser into the soil and then carefully flatten it down with my hands.

Perfectly happy.

So this is what it comes down to. On my knees, messing about with some sweet-pea seeds, why didn't anyone tell me that from the start?

That all you need is some horse shit and a few seeds. A spade. A bit of warm soil, warm the way the soil is in Finistère.

Even in February the soil is kindly and warm, you don't turn blue and freeze solid.

Your hands don't get chapped with the chilblains that used to be called cutblains when I was a child.

The soil here is balm for the hands, moist and rich.

The fields and meadows, the sunsets, the stone walls.

The ivy, the luminous moss in the woods, the paths.

The explosion of greenery in the gardens, the white winter flowers of the magnolia, the mimosa, the damp warmth of the earth in Finistère.

This bewildering happiness that has become mine, everything my hands can feel and my eyes can see.

The marvellous children with their radiant smiles, the eye contact. "*Bonjour Madame!*"

The little town with its bars. Shopi, the post office, the council offices, the cinema, the bakers, the petrol pump, the newsagent, the optician, the dentist, everything anyone could ever need is to be found in my town.

All I had to do was come here and it became mine.

The ocean, the marvellous ocean I can see from my study. The Atlantic that comes in and goes out on its enormous tides. The glittering dangerous sea and its deep trenches.

I love Finistère, all of Finistère, each and every one of its 6,733 square kilometres, I love every single one of its 283 municipalities, all of it is mine and I am shot through with love for it.

Even for the moles, the invisible moles with their little hills in my garden, the moles whose tracks terrify me — they'll overturn my peonies from below.

I even love the moles.

Here I am on my knees rooting around in the soil, happy as a field-mouse, when Madame C arrives in her purple Peugeot and stops by my fence.

Madame C is a widow.

Twice. If she got married again and her husband died, it might look suspicious, but as it is she seems to have had her fill of grief. I've no intention of marrying again, she has said with an ambiguous smile. *En passant.* That doesn't stop you being a woman. She says.

Madame C gets out of the car as elegantly as ever. She's wearing boots today, a trenchcoat and headgear that would look absurd on anyone other than Madame C.

"What are you doing?" she asks in puzzlement when she sees me with the fork and teaspoon.

"I am sweet pea," I reply, waving the package of seed. *Pois de senteur. Spencer écarlate.*

"You're sowing sweet peas," Madame C says. "Sowing seeds, planting," she goes on in that lovely way she has of teaching me her language using synonyms, *cultiver* is another word for growing plants.

We're still not on first-name terms, and we haven't started on the cheek-kissing. Madame C and I have known each other for six months now and I hope this means that things will stay the way they are.

No cheek-kissing.

I tell my Swedish friends that Madame C is my best friend in Finistère.

It's simpler that way. Though Madame C is not a best friend in the sense of an intimate confidante and her name is no more Madame C than mine is *I* — let's leave it at that.

I am not the *I* that exists in the mundane world. Madame C is not Madame C, and whatever else she might be — a best friend she is not.

★

In the beginning I always chose the most neutral word whenever I wanted to say something. Not just because my vocabulary was limited but also because I didn't want to reveal my crude character. I'm a much more cowardly creature than Madame C, much more compliant. Not only because that's my nature, but because I was born Swedish.

When my application for a mobile phone was turned down on the grounds that I am a foreigner, I said to Madame C that the loathsome saleswoman, that appalling stain on Finistère, was *not very nice*.

"You mean horrible," Madame C said, and went on to escalate the synonyms: "Appalling. Vile. Loathsome. *Terrible. Dégoutante. Déguelasse.*"

Madame C may look like a sweet pea, but she's as sharp as the diamond that glitters on her flawless hand.

This is the day in February when, on my knees sowing seeds and loving it, I say life in Finistère is so wonderful that one should write a book about it.

I get up, stretch and say one should write a book, that's how lovely it is.

Madame C takes this literally. Claps her hands, crushing my unthinking words like a fly between her palms, and exclaims that it's a brilliant idea.

"A book about Finistère, about your encounter with Finistère, *c'est génial.*"

Charming Madame C with her lovely, manicured hands and the diamond ring she was not given by one of the two men whose widow she is, those evocative gestures of hers.

"*C'est génial,*" she repeats.

"You must write a book about your first year in Finistère."

I know that I have to say no, but try doing so to Madame C! You have to say "*non*" and that doesn't help. Madame C is a very stubborn woman.

So am I.

"*Non, Madame C,*" I say. "*Non, non. Non pas. Non.*"

My first year in Finistère! Madame C, you can hear for yourself how impossible it is. Out of the question, Madame C. What the world needs is a survival handbook, not another book about some imbecile who leaves home and is astonished to discover that people talk funny and that the plumbers are unreliable.

Non, Madame C, that's not on.

I'm a serious writer. A poet is what I am, not a my-first-year-in-Finistère dilettante.

The fact that those Provence pests and Brittany blighters don't get lynched by the natives simply goes to show how kind-hearted they are.

Let those Epicurean imperialists in their straw hats live on Beaujolais nouveau for a couple of years and then banish them for ever, but don't drag me into it.

"*Non pas Madame C.*"

Whatever Epicurean imperialists might be in French, my "*non*" is a "*non*" no-one could misunderstand.

Madame C always understands what I say. For six months now she has understood what I meant and disregarded what I've said, but now it suits her not to.

There can be no question of not writing the book or of my not being the one to write it. In my own language, of course – *naturellement* – my language and my exaggerations, those exaggerations whose importance Madame C cannot emphasise enough, but since it will be a bestseller it will be translated into all the languages of the world.

"Un bess-cell-air'r," says Madame C.

Like my French, her English transcends all rules of pronunciation and syntax.

I curse my unthinking words, these words that rule my life. The words always controlling me instead of the other way round; those damned words.

"So we're agreed," says Madame C. She gathers up her rustling coat like an evening gown and glides into the car.

"See you tomorrow. *À demain.*"

"*À demain, Madame C. À demain.*"

I look at my garden, at the house, I hear the sea, the sighing of the wind in the tree-tops and the warning buoy. I feel the cool breeze off the sea.

The house, the beaches, the cliffs, the paths, the meadows. My precious freedom just to be, to cultivate my garden, to water it. I've got it all and what do I do but give it away, promise to expose it, put it up for sale. I'm betraying everything, myself as much as Finistère.

Putting feelings into words is making the natural unnatural. As anyone who has ever tried to write a post-card knows, writing is a diminution of experience, the invalidation of the obvious.

The perfectly plain.

Yet each man kills the thing he loves, it's been said, so I've promised to kill my Finistère with words.

I can't blame Madame C, but I must.

Postcards from Finistère

Madame C lives a couple of villages further inland. Her village is prettier than mine, though mine is closer to the sea. Neither of us wants to swap.

The village where Madame C lives is a fairy-tale idyll. Postcards of typical old villages in Finistère always show Madame C's village. Her village consists of a group of ancient stone buildings overgrown with ivy and wild vines, wisteria and honeysuckle. Gardens with flowerbeds filled with daffodils, hollyhocks, poppies and hydrangeas. Even a hydrangea-hater like me has to admit how lovely it is. Clouds of blue or pink hydrangeas, the most magnificent hydrangeas in all of Finistère. Huge old trees – ash, oak and lime. Wonderful plane trees. Clumps of metre-tall grass dancing like dervishes in the winter winds.

When I arrived a year ago and drove past Madame C's village, all I could see was the postcard-village with its postcard-hydrangeas and postcard-poppies. But the more you see of a village and the more you know about what lies behind its ancient walls, the more it changes from a postcard-village into a real one.

In the house next door to Madame C lives a couple in their forties with three children. He drinks and she screams and the children run around. Madame C has tried intervening in her discreet way, but has got nowhere. Between the two adults is a link that cannot be broken.

It's for the children's sake that Madame C gets involved. She's made it clear to the three of them that they're welcome at any time of the day or night. Her gate is always open.

They politely and cheerfully accept the juice, fruit or biscuits Madame C offers them. But they don't turn to her for help. The strange thing is that they are neither disturbed nor frightened. When the parents insist on proving in their peculiar way that they can't live without each other, the children run around the yard, throw balls, play with the dog or with the other children in the village.

Should they happen to be at Madame C's when the parents can be heard howling their mad scenes, the children roll their eyes and say, "There they go again." In any case it soon blows over. Or it goes on for a while. Like one of the storms that suddenly come up here, there's thunder and lightning for a while and then it's over. Or else it continues for longer than expected.

The family with the father who drinks and the mother who screams ought to be a problem family with problem children. But it's not.

When I use this as yet more evidence of how wonderful everything is in Finistère, Madame C says that conclusions of this kind are "idiotic simplifications of complicated cause-and-effect relationships".

"Though," she says, firmly, her diamond ring glittering, "if it fits in with your notion of Finistère, you must write it that way."

Madame C develops her argument further, no literary expert could have a keener eye for the difference between real life and its counterpart in fiction than the constantly surprising Madame C.

If the depiction of my Finistère is to be idyllic then I shouldn't avoid simplification, she asserts. A simplification that is idiotic in reality may radiate intelligence when presented as literature. Reality with all its complications is one thing, complication in its portrayal is another, and only the person doing the writing can determine the appropriate degree of simplification or complication.

The book is the book, reality is reality, and never the twain shall meet, as Madame C puts it.

The main thing is that the writer is clear about what's what. I'll have to use my imagination to find a solution, Madame C says, but her words fall on deaf ears.

Once she mentions "idiotic simplifications of complicated relations of cause and effect", I hear nothing more of what she says.

She's right.

It's the image of a village I'll be conveying, the superficial picture on a postcard. Not the village itself because that can't be done.

For a village to acquire depth, you have to live in it all your life. You have to know how the sediment of the generations has been deposited under the foundations of the houses, who betrayed whom fifty years ago, who has had whose children, who is whose sister, who is whose brother.

The real depths of a village can never be known to a

passer-by, and – given my experience of villages – I'm tempted to say it's just as well.

As for the description of Madame C's village, I'll leave it until some future date.

There's plenty of time to think about what image I'm going to convey. Anything's possible. Thanks to Madame C I'll be doing my utmost not to draw conclusions from superficial observations, "idiotic simplifications of complicated relations of cause and effect".

The Old Ladies' Town

On the outskirts of town there's a neighbourhood I call the old ladies' town. Because of the old ladies always standing there, talking by their gates.

The ladies talk, sweep the pavement, dead-head flowers and pick dried leaves from their magnificent plants.

At one of the houses there's a wisteria that takes everyone's breath away. Pale violet-blue, weighed down by luxuriant bunches of flowers with the scent of sweet peas. The foliage is bright green, lush and perfect. This wisteria is the wisteria to end all wisterias and its trunks climb all over the garden. Shimmering like silver, its mighty stems snaking along the fence to vault over the gate like a circus artist under the big top, the wisteria continues to the house, where it climbs all over the façade.

The wisteria must have lived for a generation at least. The houses look younger. As though the architect designed around the wisteria when the neighbourhood was being developed. The kind of wisteria I've dreamt of having around my house, but Madame C cautions me against it.

As my garden is so small – it's Madame C who says it's small – the wisteria would deprive other plants of nourishment. Nothing has such powerful roots as wisteria, *les glycines.* It can overturn an entire house, an entire village, it can split rocks.

Madame C warns me *sérieusement* not to plant wisteria in my *petit jardin*.

I'm going to have to be content with enjoying other people's wisteria and so I am.

I would never have believed I'd become one of those people who pine for a wisteria. It's like rock gardens. A rock garden – over my dead body – with rock garden plants, how boring and spinsterish. And now I take pleasure each day in my rock garden and its cactus flowers.

Every day I drive past the old ladies' town as slowly as possible without stopping while reverently admiring the wisteria.

The old ladies regard me and my car with suspicion. When I look in the rear-view mirror, I always see them turning round, carefully inspecting my foreign number plates. It'll be interesting to see whether they'll look less suspiciously at my car when its *immatriculation de véhicule* is ready and I get my Finistère plates.

The old ladies are old the way old ladies get old in Finistère. No-one passes on before the age of ninety-five. I know because I never skip the obituaries in the local newspaper.

That's the kind of old lady I'm going to be, in a dress and lace-up shoes and my hair in a bun like Grandma. Standing there chatting by the fence with Madame C until we fade imperceptibly away. Like the old ladies in the old ladies' town.

Even during the rains last winter they could be seen by their fences talking under umbrellas. This standing by fences, this sweeping of pavements, this eternal talking, that's possible because the great cold never comes to Finistère.

Your breath doesn't turn to ice here, the cold doesn't bite. The lobes of your ears, the tip of your nose, don't get deep-frozen. Your tongue doesn't freeze solid before you can get a word out. Words are few and far between in that kind of cold.

Grandma could never stand talking by her gate, there are no gates up there. They're not needed, the cold's enough of a barrier and hoar frost sets up barbed wire around the houses.

People in warmer places are able to be more open because conditions allow it. Being open where I was a child was only possible when you had brushed the snow off your boots with the broom and closed the doors behind you – the doors to the entrance hall, the inner hall and the kitchen.

There isn't much openness left after all that closing.

"Don't let the cold in" was the most common rebuke when I was a child. *Tcjlepp int in tjårrda.* I have never heard that kind of fricative in any other language and I've no idea how to write it. No orthographic system could be invented, there are no letters to describe the way that sound is formed. In order to produce it, the tongue has to be rolled up backwards and the sound pushed out through the corners of your mouth. No-one born outside the village where I grew up can pronounce this *tcj*-sound, which is just as well.

My father tried for fifty years but was no closer to getting it right when he died than when he arrived. He tried talking to the farmers in the farmers' tongue and the farmers laughed at him, both to his face and behind his back. He wanted to be one of them, but that was impossible as he wasn't from there.

There's nothing worse for a child than people laughing at her father behind his back.

Whenever my sister made drawings of ladies during our childhood she'd always draw one leg at each end of the dress. A head and the dress, and at the corners of the dress, the legs. Exactly like the old ladies in the old ladies' town in Finistère.

That's the kind of old lady I'm going to be, and it will be interesting. Death isn't in my plan. Now that I am finally beginning to get used to having this body, dying would be an absurd waste. Dying in Finistère at just the moment I've started to put down roots would be an irony I'd fail to appreciate.

At last I'm able to stand firm, legs like poles in the ground, bottom in the air. From the inland areas and mountains of central Norrland to Finistère, there are old ladies with their bottoms in the air pulling weeds, there's always something the earth needs you to do.

I used to think of getting old as a cowardly injustice against people when their resistance was down. I used to think of old age as a violation.

Now I follow with curiosity what's happening to this poor body which has been so reluctantly subservient to my will for so many years. This poor face, all the threats to it to which it has capitulated without a fight. All the unpaid work I've put into making myself a woman, all the money wasted. All those double-binds indefatigably interpreted and applied.

"Sleep with your hands raised and they'll get smaller."

"Anything you put on your face you should put on your throat."

"Wash your face with water and you might as well splash acid on it."

This war I've fought with my body, this congenital contradiction between mind and body. I'm loyal by nature, my body's a flighty fool that has, for a moment of pleasure, betrayed everything I hold dear.

The war is over now, I've won and I congratulate myself on the victory even if it was rather late in coming.

Ninety years of Palmolive soap and hard water and Grandma's cheeks were like rose petals, Grandma was smooth all over and somehow unused throughout her long old age.

Soon I'll be there, my face ravaged by skin-cream; soon my appearance will be as old as my soul.

Or the other way round.

The old lady who has been accumulating experience and wisdom inside me for all these years is coming out into the light; this wise creature is getting closer by the day.

Bonjour Madame! Bienvenue.

Or maybe not.

Madame C has a lover called Ryszard.

The *Rosenkavalier*

"One thing is certain, the first to enter the pearly gates will be the gardeners."

So it says in an article about gardening dated 1664 and that's what I used to believe. The person who gardens is free from sin. A gardener is a peaceful individual who believes in live and let live. I took this for granted until I became a gardener myself and until the day Monsieur Le R showed his true face.

Monsieur Le R is a retired widower who moved to one of the departments bordering on Finistère.

His garden was the subject of an entire spread in the gardening magazine *Le Jardin*. The garden Monsieur Le R has created is a gardener's paradise, a veritable Garden of Eden according to *Le Jardin*. This celebrated garden is situated by a small river, surrounded by woods that protect it from the wind and hills that block the winter weather.

Monsieur Le R's garden is not exposed to storms and salt winds from the sea the way the gardens in my village are. Just how exposed I didn't realise until the great rains in the winter of 2000-2001.

It's before the move, in the summer of 2000, my first summer in Finistère, that I spend a lot of time with Monsieur Le R.

Before I move into my house, before I get to know Madame C.

The garden Monsieur Le R has created with his own hands is a miracle of horticultural discipline. Geometrically shaped hedges, man-high hydrangeas, hanging baskets filled with lobelia that frame his gate.

Every plant shines, not a leaf is out of place. Not a single greenfly, not the tiniest ant. Flowerbeds straight as arrows. The plants you can never get to grow straight as arrows anyway, according to Monsieur Le R.

The only thing to be done with the pre-existing garden was to dig it up. It was entirely overgrown, a veritable jungle.

The only thing missing was the monkeys, according to Monsieur Le R.

I'd like to say that I'd be happy for my garden to be a veritable jungle, but the syntax is too complicated.

I say nothing about my jungle to Monsieur Le R. He's sweet, a bit like a little monkey himself actually. A long gap between his nose and his mouth. Short hair, small ears. About my age, only a man.

We meet at a rose nursery in the area where Monsieur Le R lives. I am doing research. I have found my house and my garden but will not be getting the keys until August.

The expectation that fills me feels like falling in love, the first stage of a romance, problem-free, all senses heightened.

I'm looking at roses to decide whether it will be a rose hedge or a laurel hedge that will enclose what will be the first garden of my life. If it's roses they will have to be the kind of roses that bloom twice a year. A rose that flowers twice is called *remontante*.

Remontante.

Rrremontante, rrremontante.

Rolling their R's is something the French do naturally. A person from southern Sweden might manage it, but for anyone from the inland areas and mountains of central Norrland, Cultivation Zone 7, it can't be done.

Just as I'm walking round the rose nursery rolling my R's, I feel someone touching my shoulder, a discreet tapping as though on a human door. A damp nose pants against my leg.

It is Monsieur Le R and his dog, the dog panting, Monsieur Le R tapping, saying it looks as though I could do with some help. He would be glad to oblige, he says.

I thank him and our relationship is a fact.

From the moment Monsieur Le R asks if I need help to the moment we sit in his pergola in the heat of high summer and he reveals his true nature, we have a relationship.

A sexual relationship?

Only if the word *sexual* is used in its broadest sense. If by sexual is meant not just the more or less pleasurable couplings of human beings but also the coming together of soil and plants, the sexuality of stamens and pistils, the sexuality of bulbs in a garden.

The encounter between a person and a garden can contain more sexuality than all the acts of intercourse women of my generation endured in order to be part of the sexual revolution.

The relationship between Monsieur Le R and me is strictly horticultural.

So far.

Monsieur Le R is a man of common sense, some of which he shares with me. Nothing is too much trouble. He gives me advice about the care of the plants from which I will get cuttings, he will even help me with grafting. He points out which plants want sun and which ones shade. He emphasises the advantages of woodland perennials as opposed to annuals and biennials.

He is unflagging, my Monsieur Le R.

In his chalk-white Citroen he takes me to flower shows, château gardens and a camellia festival, for which I thank him in an exaggerated way.

All these thank-yous are a poisoned inheritance from the land of my fathers and from my mother tongue.

"Thank you for the camellia festival, Monsieur Le R, it was unforgettable, thank you so much, thank you."

All these thank-yous for being punished when you've done nothing – thank you for the memorable camellia festival. I've been given a souvenir to last me a lifetime, one I'll never be rid of.

The crowds and the heat, the canned music from loud-speakers, French ballads and Belgian techno-pop, Celtic bagpipes. The dizziness, the nausea, the toilet that was a hole in the concrete floor.

"I can't thank you enough, Monsieur Le R, *merci beaucoup*."

After which Monsieur Le R cannot come up with enough camellia festivals to take me to in his chalk-white car.

"Soon the hydrangea season will be here, with its hydrangea festivals," Monsieur Le R says, looking at me with an expression on his enchanting baboon face that could only be described as tender. He's making plans for our future. I'm touched.

Monsieur Le R teaches me not only which plants are most suitable for planting but also about the pests and diseases that threaten them. From the moment a plant has been put in its place, it's vulnerable to threats and attacks. From without, from within, from every which way, from genetic predisposition, cellular degeneration, exhaust fumes, environmental pollution.

The plant gets attacked from the soil, from the air. The slightest breath of wind brings infectious pests from alien gardens into your own, which is stricken by epidemics and withers away.

Flying vermin, creeping, crawling, wriggling.

Ants – black ants, red ants, large ants and small ants.

Aphids, root flies, flea-beetles.

Rats and mice, voles – rodents of every kind. Snails and slugs.

Mould, moss, mildew.

Worms, fungi, viruses – from the moment you plant your first plant, it is under threat.

Everything that comes from outside is a threat to your garden.

The first thing Monsieur Le R had to do when he took over his garden ten years ago was to don protective clothing and, with a tank on his back, spray every square millimetre with a product he blends himself.

"I looked like the first man on the moon," he says, proudly.

I'm impressed.

The relationship rolls on along old and familiar lines.

There's only one pest Monsieur Le R can't control. Of all species, everything that lives and creeps and crawls, flies and runs, of all that is above and below the earth and that can threaten a garden, there's only one creature that can't be overcome even by Monsieur Le R, and that is the mole.

"Moles are the worst," he says, "and they're even worse in Finistère."

"What do I know about moles?" I say and smile at Monsieur Le R.

The relationship between Monsieur Le R and me has reached the stage where it's time to take it further, to deepen it. The relationship has arrived at the crossroads where I'm starting to wonder if it won't soon be time to switch from "*vous*" to "*tu*".

Since I'm a woman — a gender role I perform magnificently whenever we meet — I assume that it's my responsibility to suggest this.

But I hesitate.

One thing will lead to another. If we start calling each other by our first names, it won't be long before the cheek-kissing starts. This is not only customary in Finistère and its neighbouring departments, this complicated method of meeting and parting is employed throughout France.

No matter how often I see it happen, how much I try to understand the principle, I can't work out which cheek you're meant to start with. Nor what determines how many kisses should be dispensed, whether it depends on the occasion or the degree of relationship, sex or age. Whether a farewell at a railway station requires more kisses than an everyday encounter at a supermarket like the Shopi branch where I have my *carte de fidelité*.

Kisses on the cheek are given and received according to an arcane set of rules. It seems to resemble the mystery of the tides – an outsider is unable to grasp the principle no matter how often he looks at the tide tables.

There'll be no relaxing of the formalities, no deepening of the relationship. Before my hesitation can be transformed into action, the end comes for Monsieur Le R and me.

It's an afternoon in the middle of summer in the year 2000.

We're sitting in the perfect pergola he has constructed from prefabricated components. Right angles, wood treated against mould and vermin, climbing plants without the slightest blemish in perfectly vertical cascades – I sit with Monsieur Le R in a cloud of luxuriant greenery.

Butterflies flutter like petals, birds twitter. Breezes carry the scent of roses. The mimosa and magnolia are in flower, forsythia, roses, hydrangeas, everything is always in season in Monsieur Le R's garden.

On the table there is a carafe of rosé with two glasses and a bottle of Perrier.

The dog sleeps in the shade. It looks harmless, though had it not been for Monsieur Le R, it would have jumped me on more than one occasion. As it is, it's dreaming and drooling under an acacia.

It's a day of paradise in the pergola.

I'm sketching out a plan for my garden with pen and paper. Sketching is freedom, no-one ever gets closer to utopia than in a sketch. What happens afterwards remains unknown. There are no pests in a sketch, no problems. No molehills, no workmen, no price of water in Finistère.

I abandon myself to my expectations, I revel in them in a very un-Swedish way. In my homeland you're not meant to borrow against the future, you end up in debt to yourself if you do.

There are people who cling so tightly to their negative expectations that they lose their identities and kill themselves when something turns out right.

It's lovely to sit sketching in Monsieur Le R's pergola, the atmosphere is relaxed. To talk or not to talk, no demands. Monsieur Le R is one of those people who, like Madame C, understands what I mean no matter what I say, or he pretends to understand. It goes without saying that he doesn't have Madame C's elegant way of correcting you without antagonising you – he's a man, after all.

I look up from my sketch, our eyes meet. We smile at one another over the pad, he leans across to see if he can help. Where best to put the peonies, what to plant in the flower-bed facing the village road.

All the tulips I've always dreamt of having, where best to put the bulbs. How deep to plant them.

Wisteria or not wisteria, wild vines, clematis.

Rose-arbours over the gates and climbing roses on the north wall, trailing plants, the pergola – he promises to help with all of it. Everything I've ever dreamt of and an outdoor tap to water it all and a sprinkler attachment for the hose.

"And as water is so expensive in Finistère," says Monsieur Le R, pointing at a couple of enormous kegs made of grey plastic, he's going to give me barrels to save rainwater in.

"*Merci, merci.* How kind of you, Monsieur Le R, you're so kind, *merci, merci, merci.*"

Of course I don't tell him that my rainwater is going to be saved in wooden barrels with rusty hoops, the kind of barrel that stood under the drainpipes and at the corners of houses in the village where I grew up. Partly because I don't know the words for "drainpipe" or "hoop" and partly because "where I grew up" is in the past tense. Partly because I don't want to hurt Monsieur Le R's feelings.

So I change the subject. I have never asked Monsieur Le R how it was that he made up his mind to move to this department on the borders of Finistère, but now I do. Or rather, what I say is: "Why did you move the border of Finistère, Monsieur Le R?"

He understands what I mean. Despite the fact that he lives on the wrong side of the border, he understands what I mean, like Madame C, like everyone in Finistère understands.

Everyone understands what I say apart from the apprentices to the workmen who in the future will leave me in a state of impotent waiting. These young men are seized with unspeakable terror when they hear me say "stalk" instead of "pipe", or "leeks" instead of "lightbulbs".

"Leeks in all the lamps," I say, and call their boss Mr Homophile.

If it was me, I'd die, think the apprentices.

If that sort of thing can happen in Finistère, it could happen to them, they'd rather pack up their tools and do a runner than say "Mr Homophile" to their boss.

But most of the time the workmen don't turn up and that day in Monsieur Le R's pergola I am entirely ignorant of the unspeakable terror my speech will inspire in the young apprentices.

For now, it's just me and Monsieur Le R.

Monsieur Le R answers my question without even a hint of terror, without the slightest hesitation.

The reason he left, says Monsieur Le R, is that there are more blacks in his home town than in the whole of Africa. Arabs, Afghans, Albanians. Turks and Kurds, citizens of the former Soviet Union and ex-Yugoslavs. The whole map has moved there. They sleep all day and live on benefits. You can't cross the street without getting a machete in your back.

"Not that I am a racist," says Monsieur Le R, peering at the sun. He smiles at me and pours some more rosé. "Not that I am a racist, but if they're going to come here, they should at least learn the language."

There I sit, at a loss for words in his flowering pergola. Even if I knew what the words were, I wouldn't be able to find them — confronted with that kind of conviction, I would be struck dumb, whatever the language.

My head feels numb and hollow, but my body is ready to fight.

I'm on the verge of the speechless person's only means of escape — violence — but since that particular door is closed, I get nowhere. All this repressed rage, that's what it means to be a woman of my generation with my background.

A vicious circle of speechlessness closes around me, without words I can't break free, I'm gasping for breath, my eyes fill with tears, my face turns purple.

Monsieur Le R, who gets aroused by all this tearful feminine helplessness, tries to take me in his arms; I manage to get to my feet, the dog wakes up puffing and panting, I run to my car and drive off, never to visit Monsieur Le R's garden again.

In the rear-view mirror I see the dog, standing on its hind legs howling while Monsieur Le R swings his arms baboon-like, completely clueless.

I then spend the entire evening in a World War II bunker looking out at the sea. The tide is coming in, the sun sinks into the Atlantic with a blood-red sizzle.

I'm a creep, a quisling, a collaborator, a fellow racist.

Many is the evening I spend sitting at my desk or in my pergola poring over a dictionary in an attempt to write a letter to Monsieur Le R. But I turn out to be just as incapable of putting together a letter to Monsieur Le R as I am of writing the book I've promised Madame C.

You can't just drive over to his garden and shoot him, you can't even throw a stone.

Only he who is without guilt can cast the first stone, the last person to cast the first stone is me.

The Sultan and the Cucumber

In the middle of the fifteenth century Byzantium was conquered by Sultan Mehmet, Mehmet the Conqueror, the Tulip Sultan. Constantinople became Istanbul, Byzantine heads rolled, the last Byzantine Emperor took his own life.

The Turks were known for their brutality, but that they were also one of the world's most highly cultured peoples wasn't yet apparent. And a tulip had never been seen.

Europeans who went to Istanbul were astonished by the Turks' combination of bloodthirstiness, cruelty, tolerance, poetry and horticulture. This European shock at finding that other cultures have culture, that a flower as marvellous as the tulip could come from Turkey.

Sultan Mehmet with his passion for bloodbaths and tulips would amaze the already astonished Europeans.

The Sultan's palace, Topkapi – the Abode of Bliss – was decorated with precious stones, pearls, gold and silver, his harem was beyond compare. But what was most astonishing, the most miraculous thing in the entire Abode of Bliss, were the gardens.

Sultan Mehmet had more than sixty gardens. Sunken gardens, raised gardens, terraced gardens, private gardens and public parks. Orchards, kitchen gardens. Tulip gardens.

Fresh water flowed in all the Sultan's gardens – crystal-clear and cool as the best champagne. And free.

Sultan Mehmet loved to see plants proliferate, fruit and vegetables ripen, and could even be seen on his knees tending his plants himself and pruning his shrubs.

Gardening or bloodbaths, Sultan Mehmet went in for both with the same fervour; a withered flower-head fell as easily to his secateurs as the head of an enemy to his sword.

The notion that the cultivation of plants might go hand in hand with humanism was as alien to Sultan Mehmet as it is to Monsieur Le R.

Unlike Monsieur Le R, Sultan Mehmet had countless gardeners in his employ. The Sultan's gardeners were the best in the country, they had been carefully selected for their particular talents.

Like my Mademoiselle J.

Since it's impossible for me to deal with all the work the garden entails, Mademoiselle J comes every fortnight to cut the lawn and do other jobs. It was Madame C who put me in touch with Mademoiselle J, they're related in some way I don't fully understand. It must be the same way here as in the village where I was born – there are a couple of clans and everyone belongs to one or the other of them. No matter how distant the relationship – the clan you belong to determines your identity.

When I ask Madame C how she's related to Mademoiselle J, she says that genealogy is not her *cous-cous*.

When something fails to interest her, Madame C often says "That isn't my *cous-cous*." Whether this is a common expression or one she has picked up from her sons, I've no idea. Madame C and those three sons of hers I've never met.

The youngest, Benjamin, is a musician — a *rappeur*, according to Madame C, and has a vocabulary all his own.

Mademoiselle J is from a harbour town a couple of kilometres up the coast. She's spent her whole life in Finistère, twenty-three years, and has never longed for any other place.

"I too long not," I say, "for other after Finistère."

"But your family," says Mademoiselle J, in a worried, indignant tone, "what about your family?" I'd like to answer that my family will be coming to visit as soon as the guest room is finished, but the future tense isn't my *couscous*.

Mademoiselle J is both capable and reliable, as skilled at reading a garden as I am at reading a book. When something goes wrong she knows what to do — usually nothing. Nature looks after its own.

"You have to trust in Nature," Mademoiselle J says. "You mustn't intervene until it's absolutely necessary."

This orthodox belief in the earth is something Mademoiselle J shares with my father the organic farmer, and I tell her so.

On hearing the word *father* Mademoiselle J's face lights up. Having a father, having a family and relatives, makes me more of a person and less of a foreigner.

When I eventually tell her that my father was trained to be a farmer, that he graduated from agricultural college, she stops sending me a bill. Using Madame C as my intermediary, I have to transfer surreptitiously the pitiful number of francs she takes every fortnight for transforming my rumpled lawn into an emerald-green *pelouse* into her account at the *Credit Agricole*.

Mademoiselle J is the sort of kind-hearted gardener I took for granted all gardeners were until I met Monsieur Le R.

If Mademoiselle J had sought employment as one of Sultan Mehmet's gardeners, she would have been given the job on the spot. If she had accepted it, she would have been a dead woman on account of a cucumber. Yet more evidence of the accidental nature of human birth, of how we choose neither the time for our lives nor the place. Since that day in the pergola in Monsieur Le R's garden, I've been collecting evidence of this kind.

In addition to the tulips and other flowers and plants in the palace gardens, Sultan Mehmet had cucumbers planted. Juicy green cucumbers in lavishly irrigated cucumber-beds in soil perfectly suited to cucumbers. Cool cucumbers for hot days in Istanbul. History doesn't relate whether he weeded the cucumber beds himself, or whether the cultivation of cucumbers was left entirely to his many gardeners, but it does tell us what happened to the latter.

One day it happens that one of the cucumbers is missing. The Sultan summons his gardeners. They're interrogated in groups, and one by one. None of them knows anything about the vanished cucumber. None of them has taken it, they're all innocent, all of them deny the crime. The Sultan refuses to let matters rest. The cucumber's gone, it's not there. It was there but has been removed, someone did this – who?

They all swear by the trousers of the Prophet, on the lives of their mothers and their children.

The Sultan stops at nothing, he tortures the wretched gardeners, castrates them, maims them, has them broken on the wheel, crucified, mutilated and burnt with red-hot pincers. None of which has any effect. The gardeners continue to protest their innocence.

Finally, the enraged Sultan decides to take off the kid gloves. He is absolutely determined to find out what happened to the cucumber. His only recourse is to split open the stomachs of the obstinate gardeners and pluck out the intestines of each and every one of them.

The story fails to relate whether the Sultan found the cucumber. That isn't what it's about.

What a story is about depends on who is telling it and to whom. On what gets emphasised and how the conclusion is presented. Like history, a story tells you nothing by itself, there's no such thing as a story by itself. It only exists when it gets told, only then does the conclusion get drawn.

That's what's problematic about a story, about history – the fact that it can be used to prove anything.

That the Sultan was a lunatic, that that was the way things were done in those days, that the world was a different place then. That things are better now that Sultans launch Scud missiles instead of personally splitting open the stomachs of whoever took the cucumber, or controls the oil wells.

Writing means diminishing, distorting, perverting and slanting; history is always written by the victors.

Human beings are too terrifying for words. Nevertheless, they go on writing just as they always have done.

> Footman, pour me some wine, for one day
> the tulip garden will be destroyed;
> Autumn will come soon, and the spring season
> will be no more.

Thus wrote Sultan Mehmet, and no conclusions are to be drawn from this.

Tulipa sprengeri

One rainy October afternoon in the year 2000 I plant the first tulip bulbs of my life.

This tulip I esteem so highly and for which I feel such respect and awe. No other species has ever had to endure so much for the sake of its beauty. Its upright purity has been besmirched with money and blood.

After the horrific battle between the Turks and the Serbs in Kosovo in 1389, the blood-drenched battlefield with its thousands of decapitated heads in multicoloured turbans was compared to an enormous bed of tulips.

Then came the Tulip Sultan and his reign of terror.

In seventeenth-century Holland, tulips became the subject of tulipomania, a speculative frenzy similar to the recent dot-com boom in the West and with a crash of the same magnitude.

I've written a book about tulipomania.

"I ought to write a new one," I reflect, kneeling in my rain gear, pressing tulip bulbs into their bed.

A tulip book worthy of the tulip, not my previous vain attempt.

When Marguerite Duras wasn't happy with a book, she rewrote it. She told the same story but in a different voice, from a different level of insight. The story of *The Lover*, the book that won her prizes and made her world-famous, she rewrote from beginning to end.

The Lover was too superficial, thought Marguerite Duras.

I'm not Marguerite Duras, but I'm inspired by her example. Only the fact that I'm already busy with a book I'm not writing stops me from immediately starting on a new tulip-book project. All the unwritten books, the plays about Albert Speer, about Nefertiti, about the wives of so-called great men, all the novels that were started but never finished, all the unwritten things that are my life.

Not any more. I'm planting tulip bulbs now.

There are special gardening tools for planting bulbs, but I like using my hands.

All those hard tools, who knows what they might do to a delicate bulb. With great care I plant thirty tulip bulbs in the bed facing the village road, just as Monsieur Le R once taught me, double the height of the bulb.

I miss his sweet little monkey face, all the happy moments we might have shared if I'd been able to find the words to convert him from racism that day in his garden.

My thirty expensive *Tulipa sprengeri* bulbs I bought at Amsterdam airport, you're supposed to buy tulips there. It was for the sake of the bulbs that I made the stopover in Amsterdam and not in Brussels, where I once found myself at the very back of a plane full of EU delegates and drunken actors from Stockholm.

At Amsterdam airport I spend a vast sum of money I haven't got on bulbs. I charge them to my American Express card. Once the fee for the engagement I've just fulfilled in my homeland has been paid, I'll have the money in my account, that blood money.

Being an author well known from television, I sometimes get invited to speak at conferences.

Sometimes I accept. Not only for the money, although if it weren't so well paid I would say no.

Having to stand at a rostrum, confronted with the eyes and ears of thousands of strangers; being the person everyone is looking at and not fainting or dying; trying to remember what one planned to say and saying it; following on from two stand-up comedians and preceding a lifestyle consultant on the programme — there are worse ways of earning your living, but not ones I get offered.

The entire fee is gone in twenty minutes.

In addition to the thirty *Tulipa sprengeri* I buy hyacinth bulbs, lily-flowering tulip bulbs, parrot-tulip bulbs, blue and white pearl hyacinths, crocus bulbs — a black crocus with a yellow interior, the rare and expensive *Crocus korolkowii*. Narcissi — sixty white, scented narcissi, *Narcissus poeticus*.

Winter arrives, this winter of rain. The flowerbeds are under water from October to February, no living thing without gills could survive this wet winter.

I mourn my *Tulipa sprengeri*.

Looking down into the black ponds, I should have planted fish.

The Red Rose of Social Democracy

The decision to leave my homeland was made for me by the Social Insurance Office – thank you Social Insurance Office.

Having spent my life defending the public good against the ever more powerful market-economy mullahs, I found myself caught in their trap. I happened to have become slightly disabled and had to ask the Social Insurance Office for support. Don't ever do that. That the Social Insurance Office in Sweden is known as the Social Insulting Office turned out to be no joke.

My relations with the SIO were terminated with a phrase that captures the paradox of today's social democracy: "If you hadn't become disabled you'd have bought the equipment yourself." That I wouldn't have needed the equipment to begin with had I not become disabled was totally ignored by the SIO.

Madame C can't understand why there isn't a permanent general strike and popular revolution in Sweden. She doesn't understand anything about my homeland, which, whenever she criticises it, I fervently defend.

In 1997 Jacques Chirac and Tony Blair met to discuss the labour market and welfare state in the new Europe.

Chirac closed the meeting by saying: "I thought that you, Mr Blair, sir, represented the British Left and I the French Right, but that doesn't seem to be so."

When it comes to turning concepts upside down, my homeland does it better than anyone.

The poorhouse is closed but the paupers remain. Your class is revealed when you open your mouth. Teeth tell who is who.

There's an ancient rule in fist-fights: never hit a man when he's down.

Forget it.

It's the ones who are down who get hit today.

Street violence doesn't come from the streets – it comes from above as it always did.

That a person without privilege, or a group, goes mad under pressure is an old story.

That anyone is shocked when people without prospects go wrong – that's the shocking thing.

The hypocrisy of people who run things – that is the violence, violence against those who depend on coupons and special offers to make ends meet, violence against children and the elderly.

Telling old people who have only just learnt how to operate touch-tone phones and happily sit pressing "star" that now they have to make their pitiful pension trans-actions on the Internet – this is unacceptable violence against the elderly.

People are lethally stressed by being forced to choose between too many alternatives too rapidly and simulta-neously. You try to use the phone; the line is dead because you haven't chosen a network. The train doesn't arrive; the franchise owner has gone bust. All those franchise owners, all those entrepreneurs picked by the powerful, those axe-murderers hired to butcher the body of society – violence, violence, violence!

There's so much everyday violence that the word has changed meanings – the violence of down-sizing, selling-out, privatisation. A violence beyond irony or shared understanding.

What happened to me at the Social Insurance Office might have happened anywhere. At a commuter-train station, at a conference on rural affairs, at a job centre, in the street. Stockholm is one of the most expensive cities to live in and one of the most segregated, it's a no-win city compared to the win-win metropolis of my childhood.

I decided to go for win-win.

Profited from the system I'm criticising. Bought and sold my apartment and made enough to buy a house abroad.

That's what I did and it's ugly. Leaving your fellow sufferers is cowardly and evil, I ran away, I split.

But not without a few words of warning to my fellow men – fellow women, as it happened – at a conference for women in the workplace.

Entertaining at the conference were two stand-up comics, a consultant in positive thinking, a philosophising policeman and me.

My speech – delivered to fervent acclaim from the audience – was an oration against those in power. Each and every one of the fifteen hundred participants agreed, hurrahed and hallelujahed. The atmosphere was wonderful, I was a television semi-celebrity. Could have been reading from *Das Kapital* or *Mein Kampf* and everybody would have applauded.

"Do something," I said. "Protest. Don't agree to agree, don't gnash your teeth.

"Put pressure on those in power, don't let things slip out of your hands.

"Let the government do their own tax returns – demand to see their accounts now that the infrastructure's been wrecked. Don't pay one penny in taxes until you know how it's used, put your tax money in mutual funds so the economists get the message.

"Because who will end up paying?" It was a women's conference, remember. "Who'll have to go back into the kitchen and give birth in a baking dish because the maternity wards are being closed?"

I said all this; they took it in. I continued: "Do something, go on strike, take your country back from the free-market fundamentalists.

"You're not cattle, you're not cows on their way to slaughter, take your lives into your own hands.

"Do what I did, but do it your own way. Don't break down, break out! Don't complain, act!

"There is something out there for you, something for everyone. A land or a landscape, a cottage left empty when Uncle Eddie emigrated to Minnesota. A potato plot and a computer, some pine twigs for the fire. Morels and blueberries. Moose, reindeer and wild geese. Misty mornings in

August, long blue evenings in spring. Something rough or romantic. Moonlight over the endless moors."

There I stood like a minister preaching salvation, like Che Guevara, like Martin Luther King.

There's no living language for that kind of incitement and if there is, it's one of the languages I don't know. If there is one, who knows where, may it come out of hiding, may it flourish and replace the old one.

"Down with me and my generation," I said. "Overthrow us!"

I had my round of applause and thanks for being such a divinely exciting, fresh and funny entertainer, the conference co-ordinators gave me a big bouquet of red roses. Those red roses, signifying social democracy, now dangle upside down from a roof beam in my house in Finistère.

An Expatriate Bore

"Expatriate" is an insult, an assault against every individual who's left Sweden. Expatriates whine about high taxes, call Sweden the land of the Middle Way, play golf in ridiculous outfits on the sunny coasts where they spend their parasitic retirement years.

Expatriate bores are muddled paranoiacs who take each and every experience as proof that protectionism and social evils are directed against them personally, who catalogue infringements committed against them by private persons and authorities such as the Social Insurance Office.

An expatriate bore is the end, the bottom, the pits, *le pire*.

It's impossible for a foreigner to get a mobile-phone account in Finistère. You have to prove who you are in so many ways that it's impossible. That many proofs that a person exists don't exist. Buying a house is nothing compared with trying to open a mobile-phone account.

Unsuccessfully, on three consecutive occasions, I show ever new documents to a nasty young woman with a plastic badge saying: "The customer is always right."

I try to explain that there's no way I could get out of paying my mobile-phone bill, Interpol would find me wherever I fled. I show her my Swedish mobile and the contract for that account.

Nothing helps. Not only do you have to produce copies of electricity bills, water bills, phone bills, copies of all pages of your passport, you must also produce your *carte de séjour*.

My having verification from the local council signed by the appropriate civil servant and with a stamp certifying that my application for the *carte de séjour* is being processed gets me nowhere. My dear local council office towards which I feel such gratitude and where I've always been more than civilly treated. Where they've helped me with the documents I needed to seek permission to rebuild the garage or put in a skylight – *permis de construire*. Not the *permis de conduire*, driver's licence, that I'm applying for. But since nobody in Finistère expects you to apply for a driver's licence to put in a skylight, that's turned out okay.

When I want to know the price of water in Finistère every effort is made to find the exact price per cubic metre in my district.

I've been given advice on health insurance, on how to change my car registration – *immatriculation de véhicule*. The fact that I ask for documents concerning Immaculate Conception makes no difference, I'm given the proper documents for registering the car. The local council office is a second home to me, but now I'm out in the cold with my mobile problem.

The nasty young woman is only obeying orders, she says, ramrod straight in her navy blue suit like a World War II Wren.

"I'm only obeying orders," she repeats.

We're deadlocked, the aggression is mounting. On both

sides, but I'm the customer. The customer's always right and she's the one who must grant me that right.

This she has no intention of doing. She doesn't look at me, or smile, she is the exception to the rule in Finistère – she refuses to acknowledge my presence. But not as much as I refuse to acknowledge hers – I've spent a lifetime in Stockholm being trained for this kind of guerrilla tactics.

I leave the shop, grateful that we're not living in a state of war.

The post on the other hand – *La Poste*.

During a visit to the old country I send myself a parcel containing used odds and ends and a couple of new pots of face-cream, expensive face-cream promising spectacular changes to the skin. When I come to pick up the parcel at my post office in Finistère it's been opened. Nothing's missing except for the expensive face-creams. A report is filed. Then follows a period during which I receive a large number of reverential letters pledging that everything humanly possible is being done to investigate the disappearance of my face-creams, I'm assured of the humble devotion of the post office, its everlasting esteem and respect. In the final letter my forgiveness is begged for their failure to trace the face-creams. Immediate restitution is guaranteed even if money, it goes without saying, can never make up for the loss.

All I have to do is collect the cash.

On several occasions I've lost my temper and let my anger spill over on to people who, in my view, were in the wrong.

At my savings bank you can get printed slips to use when paying bills. If there's one thing I've done since coming to Finistère it is – with the use of said slips – pay my bills. This bill-paying has neither increased my happiness at being here nor managed to decrease it.

Time and time again, more and more indignantly, I've stood at the teller's window demanding TIPPs. I've lost patience, I've yelled *"absurde, stupide"* at the increasingly pale young clerk, who has attempted every kind of objection to my righteous demand.

"I am TIPP, *s'il vous plait, moi* TIPP."

The queue behind me has lengthened, I've persevered, affirming the absurdity and stupidity of being denied my TIPP. Beads of sweat forming a crown of thorns along the receding hairline of the prematurely balding young clerk.

"But Madame, are you sure you don't mean RIB?"

"I am TIPP." That I am TIPP nobody in the queue can ignore.

It ends with the ill-fated clerk printing out a RIB. I recognise the slip, leave the place quietly and deposit my savings elsewhere from then on.

One thing expatriates always complain about is the complexity of Swedish bureaucracy. In my view there's no complexity, just a plain white wall. Swedish bureaucrats have all been sent on seminars where they've been taught not to react. To say "I hear what you're saying."

In Finistère it's not like that. People respond. If you're angry the response is angry, if you're worried you are met with worry.

When I receive a gigantic bunch of documents concerning health coverage for writers from the insurance office, I don't understand a word. I take the pile to the Social Insurance Office in Finistère and, extremely worried, hand it over to a lady who immediately becomes just as worried. She leafs through the papers and says that this is impossible, *C'est impossible, Madame*. But after a moment of reflection she brightens and so do I.

There is a loophole. Leaning towards me, she explains that as a resident of Finistère there's a legal way for me to get health insurance for four years providing I take paid employment and work a total of sixty hours.

We're not worried anymore, things will work out fine.

They don't. It's as impossible for a fifty-five-year-old woman without qualifications to get a job in Finistère as it is where I come from, there's no place on earth where this camel will get through that needle's eye. All I can find is a chicken factory looking for staff to clean poultry, but when I get there 650 women my age are already ahead of me.

Terrified, I look at the bunch of documents. *C'est impossible.* As I don't want to upset the lady at the Social Insurance Office, I need to calm down on my own. I need comfort, however temporary, I need retail therapy. It's on this occasion that I find "Ingrid Bergman", the hybrid rose, at a 30-per-cent discount. With "Ingrid Bergman" in a bag I drive home and dig the appropriate hole.

The worries of the day recede.

Ingrid Bergman, who gave her name to the rose, was world-famous and wealthy, yet death came and took her before her time, just as it took Jacqueline Kennedy and

Linda McCartney, the world's wealthiest vegan. There is no place to hide. Death takes you when he chooses, nobody knows the time and the place.

Completely uninsured but consoled, I water "Ingrid Bergman" copiously. When I die I don't expect a rose to be named after me. *Tant pis*, I'd rather be a potato, a handful of earth.

Le Monde

My daily newspaper has more readers than *Le Monde*.

When the circulation figures for the country's daily newspapers are published, it turns out that my local paper is bigger than all the largest Paris newspapers put together, it's bigger than *Pravda*, bigger than *The Times*.

My local paper has 790,043 subscribers, one of whom is me.

I couldn't live without a morning paper.

As one says. Without thinking.

The only things a person can't live without are water and hope.

The morning paper gives me the data to orientate myself.

The court in The Hague, the villages in Kosovo, the demonstrations in Gothenburg and Genoa; what happens in the world happens to me.

Where I grew up, people read the *County Herald* or the *County Courier*. The newspaper you chose was determined by your view of the world. The *County Herald* was for Social Democrats, the *Courier* was for Agrarians and the Right.

Everyone knew what side they were on and what kind of people were on the other side. It was all very clear. That there were two sides was obvious to the smallest child and every dog.

From the moment I knew how to read, I read the newspaper every day. From the Korean War, Eisenhower and J. Edgar Hoover to the local news. What I found wondrous in the paper was a kind of personal ad to be found towards the back —after "Births" but before "Deaths": "All congratulations on my anniversary to be withheld."

Or: "All congratulations on the imminent occasion of my anniversary are declined. Not at home."

Refusing politely but firmly to celebrate your birthday, who would do such a weird thing?

Refusing congratulations on an imminent anniversary was the very last thing I would do, if anything was worth celebrating it was the fact that one more year of childhood was over; birthdays are proof that time travels forward and not backward.

Whoever put such an ad in the paper – it would never be me.

The person who put in the ad was always an old bachelor. A solitary old man behind the curtains on his isolated old farm, and every ten years he would take out an ad declining congratulations on his imminent fiftieth or sixtieth birthday.

Wasting money on the seventieth – no point in that, as no-one turned up anyway.

If the villagers hadn't seen the old boy out wheeling his barrow, loading dung on to his dungheap, they would have thought he was dead. As it was he boiled his bitter coffee, wound the clock, read magazines in the outhouse. Wiped the snow off his shoes with a spruce branch if it was winter, swatted mosquitoes if it was summer.

Picked potatoes if it was autumn.

Year out and year in until the day he went and hanged himself. Or took off to the forest with his elk gun. Or set out on to the endless moors.

Had nobody but himself after all. Never anyone to say the potatoes tasted nice.

No wreaths please. So there will be no wreaths wasted, nothing with roses or that kind of thing. Cornflowers. Birch boughs. The entire church adorned with them.

Primroses.

Like the ones my sister and I had to pick bunches of and stick our faces into to inhale the heady primrose scent.

Until our eyes ran with tears. And swelled up. I got eczema and sores on my scalp. Because I was a redhead, the district doctor said, I was ugly but not ill.

You didn't get cortisone injections for mosquito bites when I was a child.

The only thing that would help the kind of poor creature I was was not to make an exhibition of myself, Grandma said. To be seen but not heard, to draw as little attention to myself as ever I could. No making a spectacle, no fussing.

I made a spectacle of myself in any case.

It's been said that redheads are more ill-tempered than other people. I was an unusually ill-tempered child. The fact that I was a girl was not a mitigating circumstance. A girl is called *ståscha* in my mother tongue, or *ståsche* when directly addressed.

Mercy me, *ståsche*," Grandma said, "mercy me."

*

One childhood memory is all that I have from the village. An image not to be found in any of the photographs my father developed in a cupboard, the only image from the childhood I hurried through so I wouldn't have to be so ugly and bad.

That childhood was full of primroses and lilies-of-the-valley, saffron milk caps and coltsfoot, playing marbles and racing downhill when the railbus arrived, I only realised afterwards. In my childhood I was just a passing stranger.

The one childhood memory from the village is this:

I am standing on the hill behind the Cooperative. There was a road up there, more a path than a road. You walked from the Cooperative to the sawmill or the other way round.

I'm standing opposite a big man. I know that I'm a very little girl reaching only halfway up the old man I'm facing.

I'm the one facing him. He's wearing a hat.

This man is my enemy. He's been saying something nasty to me, standing there on the path. If it was about my mother or my father, about Grandma or about Granddad, I don't remember, or what it was he said. It was something suggestive, something evil and malicious, it was about my family and it hit its mark.

I'm opposite the man on the hill behind the Cooperative and I am so angry that I spit.

I spit at the big man and I swear. I may be little, but I've got a big mouth. All the swearwords I've ever heard and all the ones I can come up with I let fly at the man up there.

His hat like a platform over us both.

I know what I am saying and I know that it's bad.

The man knows it's bad or else I wouldn't be saying it. This devil has said something which makes me have to say it. He's said something that can't go unpunished.

What the man was called, or what he looked like, I can't remember. He's not a relative of mine, a member of my clan here in the village, he's not one of us. This devil is one of the others. Those whose cattle piss in our well.

He's from the other side and has been disrespectful about my family, this devil from hell.

I spit but I might just as well have thrown stones. Bottles of petrol.

This is war and I know it's war. I know where I belong, I am one of us and I've got to defend my own.

I won't stop, I'm not giving in.

Had it been another man in a different time, had it been a city man, ignorant of the ways of village life, he might have laughed. A city man might have just ruffled my hair and given me a toffee.

Not this man, not in this village. This man doesn't laugh.

He's looking down at me from under his platform hat.

I look back just as much. Each of us on our own side of the sun, light flashes in my head.

I spit.

Whoever will be the first to leave – it won't be me. I stay standing on the hill behind the Cooperative.

The man won.

I'm a loser, a traitor, I've betrayed my own kind. I've brought shame on my entire clan. Now he can go back to his kind and tell them what wicked children the others have. They're not decent folk, those people. More like Gypsy kids, pissing in the snow, Muslims, Jews, Arabs, Macedonians, Albanians, Turks, Asians. The child was just like a Russian, she should be ashamed of herself.

He's right.

I'm a traitor and a disgrace to my entire family.

I knew it was war, but not that the firing-line went right through me, that I was standing on the border. Everyone born in a village knows that you're either on your side or on the others'. You have to be on one side or the other.

Or you might just as well set off onto the endless moors, no congratulations on my anniversary. No church adorned with birch boughs.

No lilies-of-the-valley.

I still spit. Every morning when I read my morning paper I spit. I live, therefore I spit.

I spit.

Just as I decide to write this down, I've finally found the germ of my story – the villages, the comparison between the village where I grew up and where I was an outsider and the village in Finistère where I will always be a stranger – my mobile phone rings.

I'm seized by a powerful desire to put into words the blessing and the curse of being a stranger. This is the foundation on which my book will be written. The two villages and their secrets, their languages and climates, all the conflicts that can so easily flare up and turn into war.

Belonging and not belonging.

The energy begins to flow.

If only the mobile would shut up, why didn't I cancel my Swedish mobile-phone account, why must it ring at this particular moment? It rings and rings again.

It's just as disturbing whether I answer or not — I answer.

The call is from *Aftonbladet*, a Stockholm evening paper.

A journalist wants to interview me because I am a redhead. Scientists have discovered that red-haired people are descendants of the Neanderthals and the paper wants to know what I've got to say about it.

"I don't live there any more," I say, turn the mobile off, take the battery out and throw away the SIM-card.

I have deserted and that is that.

Lemon Balm

There's a stink coming from the drains. Even before I bought the house, the first time I was here, I was aware of the smell. But since I'd already made my mind up I suppressed the fact. Since moving in, I've been less and less successful in my attempts to ignore the smell, I've held my breath and stuffed my nose with tissues, but the fact remains, the smell exists. Somewhat depending on which way the wind blows, but exist it does.

The drainpipe is situated outside the back door and leads to the septic tank a few metres away.

I usually have my evening tea on the steps outside the back door at sunset, with the door open and the television within sight. The time the evening sun reaches the steps is when news programmes are broadcast on all the channels and *Questions pour un champion*, the quiz show with Julien Lepers, that great champion of adult education Julien Lepers. Before sundown and watering time.

So many evenings with *Questions pour un champion* and the world news. But now it's not possible anymore.

I've planted particularly pungent herbs in the bed above the overflow valve: mint, thyme, lemon balm, rosemary. Lavender. The mint is as big as a Christmas tree.

It still stinks, shit and lemon balm.

The wonderful evenings are the worst.

In winter when the storms rage and the rain pours down, the stink vanishes, you can't smell it. When it could stink and bother no-one, it doesn't.

The problem is apparent when the weather's fine.

It stinks in two places.

Both at the spot for evening tea and television, and in the garage, part of which is going to be turned into a guest room. That vital guest room referred to by Monsieur Godot, the plumber, as *le coin des amis.*

The guest room, as well as e-mail, the telephone and *La Poste*, are the essential requirements for me to live here. My living in Finistère isn't supposed to create distance between my friends and me. On the contrary, when the guest room is finished and has its own entrance, toaster and hotplate, and they can come and go as they please, we'll be closer to one another than ever.

Within reach but separated by doors that can be locked.

Which is why I've put my heart and soul into *le coin des amis* – "the friends' corner". All that waiting for Monsieur Godot, the plumber. All the planning for what I'll do once he's installed the basics, I've bought paint, a sander, curtains, a sink and a lavatory. I've bought a drill and experimented with drilling into concrete. I've done everything without first dealing with the drains.

This is rash, stupid, careless and in keeping with my nature. And that of my mother. We forge ahead like tractors, rolling on like agricultural machines at harvest-time. Leaving nothing but stubble behind.

Starting up unworkable projects with money we don't

have. Rushing ahead and ignoring the consequences. Not ignoring, as we're extremely nervous all the while, but repressing the knowledge of possible consequences, ineffectively but with great energy, while doing what we do.

Sorting out catastrophes we've caused ourselves is part of the daily routine of people like us.

The fact that the drains stink isn't my fault, but ignoring it is.

I'm about to ring Monsieur G, the plumber, when I realise that sorting out the septic tank is no ordinary plumbing job, an excavator will be needed to dig up the old one and replace it.

There's an old man in Clohars who could do it, Monsieur G, with the excavator, the – according to Madame C – very expensive and elusive Monsieur G with the excavator.

I've been given his number by Madame C but since I can't afford him I haven't called him, which is just as well. One more Monsieur Godot to wait around for is one too many at this point in my life.

There's only one way to put up with the stench from the drains – to accept it. To stop trying to suppress it, stop holding my breath and my nose. To allow the smell to exist because it so incontestably does.

That's the way it smells here, it's part of the whole.

I accept it. The smell from the drains belongs here. Like the scent of jasmine and honeysuckle by the pergola, the sweet peas along the fence, the fragrance from "Madame Alfred Carrière", the old-fashioned rose, and the smell from the herbs, the mammoth mint and the lemon balm.

There's a smell of dung outside my door.

Like the smell from a dungheap, it smells natural and good.

The Pleasure I Take in Killing Little Creatures

After a heat wave at the end of May, the plants in my garden are afflicted with illness, it's as though plague has broken out.

The rose hedge has black spot, "Ingrid Bergman", "Cuisse de Nymphe" and "Madame Alfred Carrière" are crawling with greenfly, the laurel bushes have mildew, the honeysuckle has worms, beetles are eating the stems of the hollyhocks that are just beginning to come up.

The pittosporum facing the village road drops its leaves; fat, yellow and oblong, the pittosporum leaves drop to the ground like tears, and there are groups of slow-moving black bugs devouring the nasturtium leaves.

These nasturtiums that have been so much trouble and cost me so much time and space. These yellowish-white sprouts on the windowsill, these threadlike appendages to be handled with tweezers. This vast amount of boring labour and then a group of small dark creeping creatures arrives and attacks the mature plants. Slow-moving but extremely unpleasant in their silent assemblies.

The first time I see one of my rosebuds teeming with greenfly, I'm seized by a desire to kill that I didn't know I had in me. I want to choke the greenfly with my bare hands, I take it personally, I hate the little devils.

Rage I'm used to, I'm always angry. However happy I am in Finistère, my rage against those in power remains intact. But I neither want to murder the people in power nor have them murdered, I want them to stop the terror to which ordinary people are being subjected these days – I want them to vanish to another galaxy, but to murder them – no.

The aphids, on the contrary, the speckled yellow greenfly with their shifting antennae, the tiny transparent bugs with their frogs' eyes, the beetles, the caterpillars, the worms, not to mention the slow-moving creepy-crawlies devouring the nasturtiums – I want to kill, exterminate, wipe them all out. I hate them collectively and each one for itself.

My father would no doubt have had some bio-degradable and humane means of getting rid of the slow-moving bugs, some decoction or other, of mandrake perhaps. Or, like Mademoiselle J, he'd let them go on with their chewing until they stopped of their own accord.

As far as I'm concerned, the slow-moving bugs are not human so do not deserve humane treatment. If they weren't so revolting, I'd squeeze them to death with my bare hands. As it is I drive to the ironmonger's in Quimperlé to buy poison.

I buy all the poison they have and write a cheque for the total which is stupefying. Armed with six different death sprays, two boxes of deadly blue granules and liquid poison of a strength to kill off all of Europe, I set about my task.

With the greatest of pleasure I then kill the little creatures in my garden, greenfly by greenfly, worm by worm, insect by insect.

I didn't know much about death when I came, but one year with my garden and I know all there is to know.

That happiness doesn't lead to goodness is the one unpleasant surprise I've had since coming to Finistère. That happiness hasn't made me a charitable person comes as a shock.

I'm in a chronic state of shock.

Everything I could ever have dreamed I've been given, and still I'm not a good person; I'm no better than Monsieur Le R, I am Monsieur Le R.

I'm worse than Monsieur Le R, much worse, much more horrific.

My evil is premeditated, lustful, I really kill whereas Monsieur Le R's racism has – as far as I know – not passed from thought to action.

I kill for the pleasure of killing, that's what I do.

The poisons do their work.

The one thing my lethal cocktail fails to conquer is the black spot on the rose hedge, this costly hedge of "Chrysler Imperial" and "Madame Alfred Carrière".

"Cuisse de Nymphe", on the other hand, bought cheaply when the Leclerc hypermarket had its end-of-season sale, is overflowing with gigantic, creamy white double flowers. The stem is as thick as my wrist, the branches healthy and full of sap, the leaves without blemish.

"Ingrid Bergman" abounds with dark red buds, swelling, ready-to-burst buds. The foliage is dark green and fresh, the stem is straight. Not one spot, not a single greenfly.

A couple of inexpensive miniature roses have flowered

and flowered again all winter long. Now they've grown out of their pots, tripled in size and show no sign of stopping.

While the special-offer roses flourish, the expensive rose hedge from the rose nursery hovers between life and death. With every passing day more withered buds drift sadly to the ground.

Every morning, the first thing I do is check on the rose hedge and "Madame Alfred Carrière." Things progress from bad to worse; the leaves become yellower and the black spots bigger and blacker; dry and papery, the leaves continue to fall.

The nursery staff gives me advice and products to try, but to no avail. Mademoiselle J says it will pass, like the common cold, it's nothing to worry about.

I get more and more worried. Friends have suggested I get a dog. If I can worry this much about a few plants – how much worry would a dog inspire?

I'm already worried enough about how worried I'd be if I had a dog to worry about. I decide never to get a dog.

The condition of "Madame Alfred Carrière" and "Chrysler Imperial" overshadows everything. My concerns about the unwritten book vanish. The only thing I can think about is how my costly roses are doing and I've started talking to them.

Without warning it has crept up on me, just like that. I hear myself sweet-talking the roses in a nauseating voice.

"What should we do now? How are you today, dear, mercy me, how unwell and sad you look, you poor little 'Madame Alfred Carrière', what can be done for you? Cheer up, please, straighten up, that's the way. There's a good girl."

It's like hearing yourself yelling into your mobile phone when the worst thing you can think of is people yelling into their mobile phones.

There's nothing more disagreeable to me than a woman of my generation talking to the plants in her garden, but that's what I'm doing. This is how low I've sunk, so I try to reason with myself. But since reasoning appeals to reason, my reasoning has no effect on the instinct causing me to address plants as sentient beings.

Once plants are assigned feelings, it won't be long before Darwin is denied and divine Creation is affirmed.

This eternal abuse of religiosity – I've always been against it, all those collecting boxes with Little Black Sambos, all this finishing your porridge so children in Africa won't starve. What a cheat this God is with his somersaults for arguments. To make me a believer, he'd better come up with something more convincing than nailing his son to a cross and then – if only symbolically – having him eaten.

Believers say thou shalt not seek thy creator. He'll find you when the time is ripe. The hour and the place no-one knows. Your living soul needs its creator, a godless person cannot be moral.

This abuse of the word *moral*. The only mass murder I've committed is to off a few slow-moving bugs, while this hypocrite of a creator allows mass murders to occur every second and more often than not in his name. If he's so all-powerful why doesn't he do something about the Middle East? Why can't he protect his own sacred ground?

What's he up to and how can he allow my roses to suffer?

I curse humankind's eternal longing for belief.

All the same, had Madame C not arrived in her purple Peugeot with her gracious greeting — "*Bon matin*" — I'd soon have been down on my knees invoking the name of the Lord in my rose beds.

Brought back to earth as always by Madame C, I show her the diseased rose hedge and the black-spot-covered "Madame Alfred Carrière".

"Look you Madame C, what be done?"

She shrugs her graceful shoulders.

"You could always try something else that won't work against mildew either.

"If the roses are sick, they are sick, if they're going to die, they will.

"The roses don't look at all well, no-one knows what will happen.

"One can try or not try.

"People decide what to do with roses, but roses do as they please.

"That cheap ones thrive and expensive ones perish proves nothing except that this is how it is."

One must never draw premature conclusions. And never make any decisions based on these conclusions. This is the article of faith Madame C preaches while keeping an eye on the changing ways of Nature.

Annuals can flower year upon year. Perennials can close up shop after half a season. *Les annuelles, les vivaces.*

"There's no point in worrying," says Madame C, pointing at my expensive peonies.

"Those don't look too well either."

Then she gets back into her car as gracefully as only Madame C can, gathering her skirts in her hand.

"See you tomorrow," she says, and that I must devote all my energy to the book.

"*Bon courage. À demain.*"

We've had our daily rendezvous, she's gone, but the sweet-pea fragrance of her expensive perfume lingers.

"*À demain*, Madame C."

And the next morning each and every "Chrysler Imperial" is bursting into bloom.

Slugs & Speech

Slugs are the worst problem, according to Madame C.

Slugs and snails. Slugs devouring tulip bulbs, roots and petals. Invertebrate scum leaving slimy trails in gardens, those disgusting slugs – *les limaces*.

Dagens Nyheter, the despotic daily of my former country, advocates decapitation – off with their heads. That's how you get rid of undesirables, according to *D.N.*

In the inland areas and mountains of central Norrland, Grandma used ashes, raked from the stove and packed round the roots of the blackcurrant bushes. The slugs turned round and crept over to the vegetable patch – quick march.

On her manor outside Stockholm, Grandmother used beer, which she poured into soup-dishes. When a piece from her precious porcelain service got a crack in it, she'd use it in the garden. In the village where I grew up, there were no soup bowls. You ate soup from a plate – if you were lucky.

Grandmother poured in a splash of beer as bait and put the dish under her redcurrant bushes. The slugs were attracted by the smell, got drunk and drowned in the beer.

Beer was not an option in Grandma's house. Everyone in the village was teetotal and belonged to the temperance lodge, apart from four brothers who lived on moonshine and raw sausage, but that's another story.

Slugs must be put to death, no question about it. You won't have to struggle with yourself about this as you would if they were moles. The slugs must die.

To murder a mole with malice aforethought would be unthinkable, but getting rid of a slimy slug with eyes on stalks like men from Mars is a pleasure.

I once knew a girl who ate a slug. She put it into her mouth and swallowed it.

Slugs are called *åma* in the language spoken in the village where I grew up. A language all its own, not a dialect, that was my mother tongue. The language you are born to is called your mother tongue. Not just where I grew up – *langue maternelle, Muttersprache*, a "mother tongue" is a "mother tongue". The country where you are born is called the land of your fathers, *Vaterland, patrie*.

The children in the village had a bet as to who would dare to eat an *åma*. This girl was the only one who dared. The slug tasted like eggs, she said.

That's what children did for entertainment before computer games.

The same girl had seen her grandfather die. She'd been out walking with him, he'd said, "I'll just sit myself down here for a bit." And sat down on a stone wall and died.

He'd said it in the language of the village, a language that has no written form. If what he said were to be transcribed, it would roughly be: *Jä sätt mä henan lite jä.*

The *jä* that introduces and concludes the sentence means "I" and is pronounced like the English *yeah*.

Being bilingual is no blessing when the two languages happen to be the ones I was born to. The one more marginal than the other. Not that I'm advocating Esperanto, but you won't find me demonstrating in favour of preserving rural tongues.

There are quite enough Balkans in the world as it is.

The girl who'd seen her grandfather die became the most popular child in the village, while it lasted. Over and over again she had to describe what he looked like at the moment of death. The sigh that came out of him at both ends. How his chin dropped with a snap, but his false teeth stayed in place.

This sounds petty and crude in Swedish, but Swedish is the only written language to which I have access. That urban language for urban experiences, that bleak language without the colours, the contrasts and the nuances of my mother tongue.

After fifty years of speaking Swedish I still have a feeling of foreignness. As though I were trying to be someone else. The greatest crime a villager can commit is to behave like a city person.

Speaking Swedish is going over to the other side. To the rulers, the gentry.

Anyone born with a foot in both camps becomes very careful with words and gets splits in two.

In Finistère it's not like that. Here I speak my own language, with its own syntax and its own conjugations. If I did that where I grew up, I'd be considered crazy. But I don't seem to be considered crazy in my village in Finistère. An immigrant and forever a foreigner but not crazy. "Madame burns her hydrangeas and doesn't close her shutters, Madame's not from round here, so that's all right. Madame speaks peculiar but she speaks the best she can."

After much effort, I've given up any attempt to learn the language. It just won't take.

In the beginning, my aim was to learn one conjugation a day: "I am, I was, I have been, I will be, I would have been, I will have been, I will have been being, I have been being, I was being, I would have been being . . ."

I've worn out three grammar books, two of which are elementary-school level; courses on tape and the CD in the car with the new language course, Echelle, and the many little shortcuts it offers to everyday French, none of which leads to me.

After a year I know more verbs than when I arrived, but conjugate them I cannot.

It doesn't matter to me.

Speaking in the present tense — and not in the imperfect, the conditional or the future — is in keeping with my nature and the way I see things — I live in the present, the now.

Not "I would have lived, I have lived, I will live."

The fact that I enjoy listening to the wonderful language on the answering machine *chez* Madame C is one more pleasure to add to all the others in Finistère, and speaking it is not something I have to be able to do myself to enjoy it. If it were, all the fine arts could be done away with immediately.

Listening to Madame C on the answering machine is like a day at the Louvre: "*C'est Madame C à l'appareil. Je suis absente pour le moment prière de laisser votre nom et votre numéro de téléphone et je vous rappelle dès que je suis revenue. Merci pour votre appel, bonne journée."*

Enjoying something doesn't mean having to be able to do it yourself.

I harm no-one by speaking as I do, on the contrary. I make people happy. The only ones who suffer are Monsieur Godot's apprentices – they suffer unspeakable terror when I address them – but given how rarely Monsieur G turns up, the loss can be written off.

It's not as though Monsieur Godot knows how to speak any languages himself. When he calls out to me it can come out as: *Madame Msoengh! Madame Maschtan! Madame Malouse!* Though since I understand it's me he means, I come when he calls.

When my first water bill arrives in the post, Monsieur G happens to be in my house, an exception and a blessing. When I unsuspectingly tear open the envelope, I don't understand what I see. It's the first water bill of my life, on the farm in the north we had our own well, and in the flats where I lived around Stockholm, I don't recall water having a price.

I can't believe my eyes. I think the amount must be in Euros, until I realise that if it were in Euros the amount would be lower than I thought, not six and a half times higher. It's just not possible that water can be so expensive.

"Monsieur Godot," I shout. "Look you! I am an enormous bill, look you, Monsieur. I am an enormous bill of water."

You say "Monsieur" here – Mister Godot.

In Finistère they don't take coffee breaks all the time the way they do in Sweden. If you failed to offer someone coffee where I come from you'd be considered an evil person. If I hadn't offered Johnny and Olle coffee when they cleaned the pipes in our cottage in the village, the news of how mean I was would have gone round the entire region in a matter of seconds. Had I called Johnny and Olle Mister Lundgren and Mister Johansson, in next to no time the whole county would have known how stuck-up I'd become, and how like a Stockholmer.

Monsieur Godot does not take breaks. When it's hot I try and offer him something to drink with a pleasant "You a sink, Monsieur Godot?"

He smokes like a chimney.

"Do you smoke?" he asks, offering me a Gitane.

"Sight others smoking yes please no."

To the painter's answering machine: "Hello being Madame, I am forget when things you ask. The foot of the bed passed. I'm not remember."

The tape ends, new call: "Yes. It Madame again. Again. It wall, new not good I can it in French good evening."

To the painter when he arrives: "Hello, Mister M, I ask if you have very strong glues. Myself I'm only usually sticky."

"Not at all, not at all, but I afraid he collapse complete."

"Thank you very much, thank you very much, that is very kind, thank you thank you. *Merci beaucoup.*"

At the garage: "Good day! I to put gas on the cart, thank you very much."

At the cobblers: "The shoes please look. She toffee. You can?"

At the DIY store: "Pardon – how many it box sleeps?"

At the hairdresser's: "Thank you very much, thank you. What yours name? You can write?"

Names are a major problem for me, all those names that seem so similar to words with other meanings. The more aware I am of the trap, the more easily I fall into it.

At Monsieur H's, the ironmonger's: "*Bonjour*, Mister Homophile, pardon I question, the rock. Watch. It cement."

I show him my glazed tile: "It must on for water. Oh thank you very kindly, thank you thank you."

I leave with the sample, return the next day: "Good day, Mister Homophile."

"No pardon pardon thank you so much, thank you thank you."

"I ask you if this one not product."

"Thanks very kind, thank you thank you. To think about very thanks."

I come back the next day, Mrs H is in the shop: "Hello Mrs Mister Homophile."

I show her the product. "Your husband this product."

Times beyond number I call the kindly and, as I subsequently discover, deeply religious Monsieur H Mister Homophile.

Every time it happens I see his delivery boy turn pale, yet another of the young men seized with unspeakable terror on hearing me speak, and in my mind's ear I can hear his wordless prayer: "Dear Lord, don't let her call the boss Mr Homophile again."

His prayer goes unanswered.

For a long while I was a regular customer at an expensive furnishings shop 20 or 30 kilometres from my village. Everything I've got in the house has either been bought second-hand, on sale or there: "*Bonjour Madame*. I am the lamps. Thank you so much."

"And the toastbreader. Iron made. Thank you so much."

"No, not thanks. Look a little one before."

"Also want on the wall, thank you."

At the fabric and wallpaper counter: "Excuse me, sorry. How many cost this?"

"Applies to the rags also the 14 per cent?"

"Are you American Express?"

"Yes, it have. It goes well on sack."

"Thank you very much, yes. I am the cart outside. Happiness leeks that way. Not like modern, small. Modern leeks very difficult. I am fortune they like this."

Screwing motion with my hand: "I don't understand me! Why change leeks?"

"Thanks so much, thank you thank you, *au revoir*."

In this language all my own I've bought an entire house with attached garden. I've managed to take out insurance policies, had the car – "the cart" – repaired, as it's always scratched when you come out of the supermarket, which is part of the culture here. I've even scratched a car myself and told the owner off for being careless. He looked so stupid standing there staring at his scratch.

"I don't understand me, if you please," I said, and drove off.

I've been to the dentist, the local council offices, the Social Insurance Office and the tax office, and in all likelihood my car will get registered despite the fact that I've applied for Immaculate Conception on its behalf.

The Finistèrians understand.

Madame C in particular, of course.

The only thing I don't like about Madame C is the business of the book, this unholy alliance she has dragged me into. Forcing me to profane my feelings for Finistère with something as clumsy as language.

To evade the issue, I talk at length about the extermination of slugs. And suddenly, since it's of no importance, everything comes out perfectly, the conjugation of the verbs and the syntax. *Subjonctif, plus-que-parfait, futur antérieur.*

The right words for "ash" and "beer" present themselves. "Maternal" as opposed to "paternal" grandmother – *grandmère maternelle, grandmère paternelle*. All of a sudden I am using the imperfect tense: "My maternal grandmother used to use ash, my paternal grandmother used beer."

"I'm going to experiment with both methods" – the future tense.

"I would be happy if I could get rid of the killer slugs" – conditional and subjunctive! Knowledge I must have had but couldn't access is at my disposal – I conjugate auxiliary verbs as I've never conjugated auxiliary verbs before.

It doesn't seem that Madame C notices how well I'm speaking, she doesn't comment on it.

As for herself, she uses *Anti-Limace longue durée*, she says, whereupon she asks how the book is coming along. Just like that. Catching me out in the middle of conjugating "to exterminate".

"What book?" I say. Even though this turns into "What boot?" as usual, she understands as she always does.

"*The Price of Water in Finistère*," says Madame C. "What other book would I be asking you about? *And Quiet Flows the Don?*"

The Man from Moëlan

There used to be a man in Moëlan who knew how to get rid of moles, but he died.

The man from Moëlan was the only person who knew how to get moles out of gardens and into fields and woods without harming them.

He shooed them away.

No-one knows how he did it and he didn't train anyone. The secret of sorting out the mole problem without murdering moles died with the man from Moëlan.

Moles are a problem for most people here, except Madame C.

It's not that Madame C doesn't have moles in her garden, she just doesn't consider them to be a problem.

Mademoiselle J thinks they might be a minor problem but nothing to worry about.

Moles do no serious harm, they're insectivores, not rodents. They don't eat the roots of plants the way voles and mice do. Their subterranean tunnels help to aerate the soil, which is a good thing, according to Mademoiselle J.

Since moles are part of nature, Man should adapt to the mole and not the other way round. Mademoiselle J says what my father would have said and I don't agree.

I find moles most disagreeable.

If you step on a molehill, the earth gives way. As if you're falling through the earth, like Alice down to Wonderland.

In the beginning, molehills may have seemed comical and interesting to me, but as time goes by I get more and more irritated.

Which is pointless, according to Madame C. "*À quoi bon?*"

The word for mole is *taupe*.

Although I know that the word is *taupe*, when I'm upset it becomes *tape*. Madame C understands what I mean, as always, and discreetly corrects me without making me feel I'm being reprimanded. When I'm very upset I usually say "Madman C" to Madame C.

Until I came to Finistère, I had no idea moles could be a problem in a garden. Where I grew up, the ground is too cold.

There have always been a lot of moles in Finistère. Since the man from Moëlan died, more than ever before.

Most of them in my garden.

Moles don't reveal themselves to humans. No-one I ask has seen a mole. The man from Moëlan must have done, but not my neighbours in the village. Not Monsieur Le R. Not Madame C. Not me. Until one day I'm out walking and almost step on one.

The mole is on its back with its little excavator-paws on its belly. Mole-brown. Endearing. Dead.

It's much smaller than I'd imagined, it's as small as a lemming.

The possibility of a lemming lying dead at my feet in Finistère is zero. The lemming lives exclusively in the mountainous regions of northern Scandinavia. A dead lemming on a path in Finistère is a complete impossibility. There are no mountains in Finistère.

Once, when I was a child, a migration of lemmings passed through the village. Thousands of lemmings that had been gathering at the tree-line arrived in procession, a caravan of lemmings of which neither beginning nor end could be seen.

The lemmings were on their way from the mountains to the sea.

Why the lemmings started walking, whether there was a lemming-leader, or whether it was a collective instinct that got them going, nobody knew. Or whether it was starvation or other threats.

Various theories existed as to why the lemmings abandoned their safe dens, but why they committed collective suicide I've never managed to discover. Because when the lemmings arrived at the sea, they didn't stop. They didn't come to a halt at the beach, they didn't settle there and build dens in the sand, forming lemming families and having lemming children.

They kept on going.

Straight out into the Gulf of Bothnia.

From the mountains to the sea they walked as though following a compass. Across streams, country roads and villages. Without pause, the lemming migration marched day and night, straight to their collective death. Without anybody knowing why.

Survival is the most powerful instinct in animals and human beings. That the lemmings didn't have it was a mystery.

On its way to the sea the lemming march never paused, leaving a trail of dead lemmings in its wake. Marching towards the sea, the lemmings let their brothers and sisters die without attempting to save them. On their way to that greater death which made the number of dead lemmings left behind in our village insignificant.

My sister and I and the other children dug little mass-graves and threw the dead lemmings into them. We sang psalms and made the sign of the cross. As a child I used to dream about being a nun, it must have been something I'd read.

The tiny corpse lying at my feet on the path in Finistère is undoubtedly a mole. All the distinguishing features match the picture of a mole in *Le Petit Larousse*. Except that I'd imagined the mole would be bigger, that it would look like the noxious beast it is. That it'd be as big as a badger, or a wild boar. Not this small, defenceless cadaver. How such a captivating little creature can cause the devastation moles bring about is astonishing. I curse the fact.

There are mornings when my garden resembles an excavation site of prehistoric graves. Grave mound after grave mound. Molehills around the trunks of the magnolias, molehills in the flowerbeds and the vegetable patch. Molehills on the lawn, you can't see the grass for the molehills. Molehills by the peonies.

I've long felt that something has to be done about the mole problem. On a rainy Sunday morning in March, I decide the time has come.

When I go out into the garden, what do I see but peonies lying on the ground, their roots in the air. My precious scented peonies. The infernal moles have upended them – this is the limit. This far and no further.

I return indoors and look up "mole" on the Internet. If a solution to the mole problem can't be found there, then no solution exists.

It does. Not one but hundreds of solutions to the mole problem. One of the less appalling ones is to put chewing-gum in the tunnels. Since the mole doesn't understand that it should chew the gum, not swallow it, its guts get blocked and the whole mole bursts like a balloon.

Another way to do it is by tying a hose-pipe to the car exhaust and directing the fumes down into the tunnels. You can order ready-made gas bombs from the US – *Giant Destroyer Smoke Bombs*. You can put down traps, each crueller and with more monstrous bait than the last.

There are ultrasonic vibrators which are supposed to make moles feel so sick to their stomachs that they die.

There are anti-mole weapons, guns, pistols, you can destroy moles with mole missiles, there are a thousand and one means of exterminating moles, but none that a woman of my sensitivity could bear to use. Searching for information on the Internet is like entering a gigantic and labyrinthine Nazi world-brain obsessed with the annihilating of moles.

I want to be rid of the problem but not to hold the weapon myself.

I damn the man from Moëlan for taking the art of shooing moles away to his grave.

The only person left to turn to is Monsieur H, the iron-monger. His shop is open on Sunday mornings. I drive there.

Monsieur H is the kind of shop-owner who will do anything for a customer. He ignores the fact that I call him Monsieur Homophile.

He's helped me find paint, plaster, kitchen equipment, hyacinth bulbs, bottled gas, an incinerator, a wheelbarrow, buckets. Products for getting rid of moss, mould, paint, ants, greenfly, and instructions on how to go about it and what quantities to use.

He's changed the blade on my saw, solved the problem of how to wax brick, he gave me telephone numbers for the bricklayer and the skylight man. If anyone can help me sort out the mole problem, it will be Monsieur H.

When I arrive at the ironmonger's, it is not yet nine o'clock. Monsieur H is busy carrying out the ladders and baskets, wheelbarrows and gardening tools that live outside the entrance to the shop when it's open. He's totally focused on his task, which he carries out meticulously.

Forgetting that Finistèrians can do anything except two things at the same time, I force my way between Monsieur H and a roll of wire-fencing.

Allowing a person the time they need to finish a job is an elementary skill here. Even at the supermarket checkout, however long the queue may be, the cashier will say to the customer fumbling for their chequebook or coins: "Take your time. Take all the time you need. Take your time."

The minimal social skills I've acquired are gone with the wind, I throw myself at Monsieur H, shouting: "Tapes, the tapes! You the help, Monsieur, the tapes."

You're not supposed to rush someone from Finistère, I'm rushing him. Monsieur H refuses to be rushed. I might just as well be a mole myself for all the notice he takes, he's got his task to do and he is doing it.

When he's finished his face says nothing, but his body language speaks volumes. But Monsieur H is a good person, he allows the irritation the time it needs, then he's his usual helpful self. He expresses regret that the legendary gentleman from Moëlan passed away without training a successor.

"Though," Monsieur H says, "there is one product."

There is always a product at Monsieur H's. The product for shooing moles away consists of lumps whose smell is so unpleasant to moles that they leave of their own accord.

A lump of this product in the opening to the mole tunnel and the mole is so disgusted that it gathers its family together and runs away, never to return.

Monsieur H puts the product in a plastic bag and warns me to be very careful when putting the product in place. Gloves are recommended, preferably protective clothing. In particular he warns against moisture. The product must not become damp. If it does it will explode.

I thank him and hurry home. The whole of Sunday is spent in setting out the lumps, which smell of sulphur and methane. The product gets a bit damp, but luck is on my side. There is no explosion.

When evening comes I go inside, soaked through and worn out, but with the wonderful feeling of a job well done.

The next morning it looks like a gang of drunken hooligans has ripped the garden to pieces. From the village road at the front to the path at the back, it's been torn apart. The remains of torn plants dangle from trees and bushes. One or two scraps of peony.

It looks like the battle of Stalingrad.

When Madame C arrives, I say that the excavator man has been here. Someone has unexpectedly sent me some money, I add.

Madame C is sceptical. She's unwilling to swallow the idea that Monsieur G, the excavator, would turn up overnight. But since she is obliged to believe her own eyes, she says that I must be living under a lucky star here in Finistère.

"Obviously."

"*Évidemment*," she says, the diamond ring flashing with suspicion on her hand.

Possessed by a Justified Feeling
of Confidence

Ever since the day at the end of February when I promised Madame C to write a book about my Finistère, I've done nothing but keep starting again.

I've begun with the background to my arriving in Finistère, my being absolutely lost where I was. In certain countries, it's the length of your beard that determines whether you can get work and somewhere to live, in my homeland it's your bank balance. But since the book I've promised Madame C is to be a happy book, it can't begin that way.

Like the first fifteen days for a plant, the first fifteen words of a story have to contain everything the story needs to survive.

If I can only get these fifteen words together the rest of the words will start to flow. If only I can get over the fifteen-word threshold, I'll be home free.

It isn't easier on the other side of the threshold, it's farther away from the feeling and closer to the deadline. Creating a sentence that is as natural as what it's meant to describe, forget it.

Putting words to an experience is like taking a lizard by the tail, the lizard runs off and there you are with the tail in your hand.

The feeling runs off and the words are left, these little dry tails.

Walking along the cliffs above the Atlantic.

Looking out over the surface of the sea. Feeling its vastness, the extent of it. Its lack of purpose. Taking it in. Being filled with this dizzying insight into how undescribable it is.

Everything I want to describe is undescribable and impossible to write.

There's nothing more to say. Nothing nothing nothing.

The only way to do it is to write a book called *Happiness Writes White* with the title printed on it, then six hundred blank pages. But that's not the kind of modernist I am.

The sweet-pea seeds I planted on that day of doom in February, the day I promised Madame C I would write the book, have turned into the fragrant screen of white, pink, purple and red sweet peas I hoped for.

The sweet peas are as tall as a man and not one word has been written.

Madame C knows nothing of this.

When she asks how the book is coming along and I avoid answering, she says "*Pardon*" with the same smile members of secret societies give one another.

She has no intention of disturbing the creative process, she says.

She puts her index finger across her discreetly but perfectly painted mouth and whispers, "*À demain*. See you tomorrow, good luck with the writing, *bon courage*."

Having made the promise to Madame C, my paradise is ruined. Not lost, only glimpsed.

The year loses its chronology, disparate images flicker between abysses of performance anxiety.

Finistère exists in my heart, in my senses, but that's it.

On the occasions when I try to get free of my promise to write the book, Madame C suddenly finds herself in a hurry. Her Polish visitor is about to arrive, it's time for her tango class, her sons are coming to see her, these sons that have never been seen. She gathers up her dress, gets into the car and disappears with an absent-minded "*Bon courage*" and "*À demain.*"

What I've promised Madame C is no great epic, we're not talking about *War and Peace*. It's not a proper novel with fictional characters, even if everything becomes fictional when it's written down. What I am going to write is a little journal, a few light notes, twenty thousand words.

More or less.

A few unambiguous words about how I found my Finistère and how I find it anew.

Not too simple, I'm supposed to be a writer, after all.

My first garden, some free and impressionistic images, no pretensions.

Head against hard-drive and my impressions could be transferred to disc. Head upended, emptied like a waste basket, and into the computer's memory.

My head is full, that's not the problem.

I've got enough material for a hundred, a thousand different books about as many Finistères; all I have to do is sort the material out, collate everything I've amassed and imagined. Everything I've felt and done has been recorded, set down in print or jotted down in a kind of shorthand. Everything noted so as not to be forgotten.

Heaps of undated notes keep piling up, jottings on the backs of receipts, torn out newspaper pages, packaging, lampshades, kitchen paper. I've cut out articles, news items, adverts and photographs from newspapers and magazines.

On the walls in my study I've stapled picture upon picture, note upon note, I'm surrounded on all sides by information I don't understand.

All these more or less illegible notes in my self-revealing handwriting — it leans strongly and decisively forward only to retreat on the next stroke.

All these fragments, this scattered wreckage of impressions, that have to be turned into a whole before they fade away.

The very first note I typed out on the computer and put up on the wall has already disappeared, the one that said:

"Possessed by a justified feeling of confidence, I begin again."

The Howling Pope

There's a cinema in my town. New films arrive just a few weeks after they've been shown in Paris. One day in October there's a film I want to see, a thriller.

The autumn rains have begun. I can think of no better way of spending a rainy afternoon than sitting in a cinema and hearing the rain outside.

When the film prizes are awarded at the end of the year, the actor who plays the psychopath in the film, Harry, will be awarded the prize for best male actor, although neither he nor I know it on this afternoon in October.

I buy my ticket, showing my *carte de fidelité*. I've got a *carte de fidelité* at Shopi, the supermarket, at Point Vert, the garden centre, at Leroy Merlin, the DIY store, at the dry cleaner's and at the baker's, I am a *carte de fidelité* snob. In the same way that the economically gifted flip through their credit cards, I flip through my *cartes de fidelité* when paying. After ten films, the eleventh one is free.

The cinema foyer is empty. After a rainy day, the weather has cleared and people are making the most of it. "Making the most of" is called *profiter*. I have to admit that profiting from the fine weather doesn't count as illegitimate exploitation of the world's natural resources.

I go in and sit down. Leaning back in my seat, row nine in

the middle, I'm filled with the priceless sense of expectation one feels in a cinema before the film begins.

When the film is due to start, I'm still the only one in the auditorium. Showing a film to 179 empty seats, simply because there's one person in the middle of row nine, even though she has a *carte de fidelité*, would be absurd.

I'm close to tears, all the disappointment in me, a river of dammed-up grief I thought myself rid of, is about to burst its banks.

"How typical," I think, "typical typical typical."

Women of my generation in the part of the world I come from react this way. As though we were more under-privileged than the rest of the world that's starving and exiled, as though we were the victims. When we're the guilty ones, the ones who are to blame for things being the way they are.

We were given every conceivable freedom and opportunity and made nothing of them. We are the generation that gave up.

I'm just about to leave when the adverts begin. Over-joyed, I sink back into my seat. Thank you, cinema!

The film is the best I've seen since Hitchcock's in my youth. Psychopaths as believable as this can only be found in the real world nowadays.

Harry's the kind of psychopath who won't leave you alone, not during the film, not afterwards.

What is it that makes him a murderer, what flaw, is it acquired or congenital? The pity you feel for Harry, mad and dangerous as he is, the pity you feel for anyone who crosses his path; the pity you feel for everyone and everything can drive you insane, and insane is what Harry is.

There's a scene in the film, it's at night, he's driving his Mercedes alone in the dark, just the headlights boring holes into the blackness, he has committed murder and is about to kill again.

Something has gone against him, there's something wrong, everything's wrong. He floors the accelerator, pushing the car to greater and greater speeds.

Faster and faster he goes, his face is distorted, the car is vibrating, he's driving in the dark as fast as a new Mercedes can be driven and he's screaming.

He howls into the night and his howl is raw and true.

This is more than a psychopath howling between murders. It's not just Harry screaming on the screen. It's the madness of the world screaming, the scream of evil, the howl of violence, of the arms trade and of weapons.

Everything that came to nothing, the wrongs I've done, the wrongs my generation has done by doing nothing. The scream is the kind of scream in paintings by Francis Bacon, where popes scream in confinement. All those Innocents and John Pauls, God's representatives on Earth with blood on their hands. My generation could have done something good, a little something, but we didn't even do that and the blood on our hands is fresh.

There was an opening, but we let it close up; we did nothing and there is no worse crime, the greatest evil is to be aware and do nothing.

The scream is our scream, it is mine, the evil that is

laziness, selfishness, I am creating my garden, I rejoice while others suffer.

Drugged children are sent into tribal wars armed with machine guns, dirty kids sit on the floor in filthy sweatshops and make trainers, children are starved and exploited – it's not as if I don't know.

I know, everybody knows, we've all seen the pictures, all the transient pictures and the ones that stick in the mind – like the one of African children whose parents have died of AIDS. It's a group portrait. The children look into the camera, their faces like the faces of orphans when Grandma was a child, matter-of-fact eyes, not begging, not asking for anything.

Whom should they ask?

It's the same impoverishment as in Grandma's time, my generation has done nothing about it, we're letting it happen again, not just in Africa, we're letting it happen all over the world, allowing it to continue.

We were the only generation who had the chance, we had the perspective, we weren't caught up in it like Grandma, not like my mother's generation who were still subject to the old ways, the poorhouse was too recent for my mother's generation.

My generation had everything, the Pill and the jobs, the bright future. My generation took the future and kept it for ourselves, looking after our pensions. We stole the future from our children, we failed to hold this gift in trust, we grabbed everything we could lay our hands on, we embezzled the future.

We could have done something, I know it would have

been possible, it was a time of possibilities, a moment in the history of the West that we let pass.

My generation is a generation of psychopaths – the suffering of other people is not real to us, we cannot feel it, there's only us and what's ours: how typical.

In the howl of the psychopath we show our true faces, the black hole in our faces, we howl because we know what we've done, it's guilt howling, the personal guilt of each and every one of us.

I sit there shaking in the middle of row nine.

To know how deep the guilt is and still go out into the sunshine, to drive your car through the villages, homewards, towards the sea, to approach your house, to have a house to approach, to send your cheques to *Médecins sans Frontières*, to pitch your penny into the collection box, to live happily in meaninglessness, because the opposite would be even more meaningless.

I am a howling pope, I am the psychopath driving my car.

The rain is starting to fall again.

A thick grey rain falls and it won't stop falling until the end of February.

It'll be four months before I see the sun again.

When I return home from the cinema, I don't know this, but I can feel it. The Flood is coming and my generation is to blame.

The Flood — *Le Déluge*

It's raining.

A persistent rain that will continue throughout the autumn, over Christmas, over the New Year, throughout January and February and into March. Days of rain will succeed one another, it will rain as it's never rained before in Finistère.

No long-term forecast could have predicted the deluge my first winter in Finistère will turn into. It hasn't rained so much since records began to be kept. My first winter's *pluviométrie exceptionelle*.

Madame C and I don't believe in weather reports.

She, because she was born by the sea, I, because I come from the inland areas and mountains of central Norrland. We are both from parts of the world where the weather does as it pleases whatever the weather reports say.

Where I grew up a hot summer day could arrive like a bolt from the blue. My sister and I would be splashing naked in the millpond among the minnows, dragonflies buzzing above us, the sky a blazing azure like a dragonfly's wing, and all of a sudden, from one second to the next, a wind would pick up that was so icy cold that we had to escape from the millpond or freeze to death.

That's the way it is.

Unreliable and violent.

The growing season is brief. Brief and exhaustingly intense.

When the light returns, it is total. The plants shoot up in shock, up from the poor soil, growing with incredible haste, time is so short.

So much light during the brief period of brightness and so much darkness for so long.

If a summer turns out to be sunny it has to be saved, bottled, dried, preserved and handled with care to last for years to come.

Intoxicated haste rules in that kind of climate.

Everything has to be put to good use, nothing must be lost, not a single blue anemone, not one mushroom.

In a summer when the mountain winds keep to the far side of the tree-line, a sunny and exceptionally precious summer, there is nothing as spectacular as a village in the part of the world where I grew up. No colours as bright, no scents as saturated, no wild strawberries as sweet, threaded on blades of grass like pieces of coral. Blackcurrant bushes groaning under clusters of berries, the smell of the black-currant bushes, the heady and perilous scent of blackcurrant leaves, it all has to be inhaled to the full.

It's miraculous and potentially lethal because it's so treacherously unpredictable and transient.

You have to have strong nerves to live up there.

The spirit has to be hardy to endure the brutal light of summer and the spectacular darkness of winter.

The midsummer light that is suddenly transformed into 35° below zero. Darkness day and night, month after month.

The breath freezes in your nose, your mouth, your lungs.

The skin gets ripped off your tongue, you can't talk in the cold, the words freeze.

There's no community, the village has no "us". Everything is closed in.

People sit by the stove with their hands stretched towards it and the stove never gets hot enough, even when it's red-hot.

There's no rest in land like that. Only the best can live there.

Those who do are no less sensitive than other people, on the contrary, they're extremely sensitive. With their senses heightened they savour the morel in the clearing, the orchids — the Black Vanilla and the Lady's Slipper — the cloudberries on the moors, the fruits of the forest. They absorb everything and make it into nourishment and energy to last out the winter.

People who live in the cold lands have, or must acquire, the capacity to store and preserve in their memories each bud, every potato, every ray of sunshine, every drop of soft summer rain.

Next year the potato flower will freeze and the barley will turn black, next year there'll be snow on Midsummer's Eve, or this very year. Everything can be ruined at any moment.

All the grown-ups in the village where I grew up were slaves to the weather report.

Everyone knew it never came true, but it was not to be missed.

The weather report was a ritual everyone took part in, it

was like the church services on the radio for Christians, like the multiple daily prayers for Muslims.

You couldn't miss the weather report.

Whoever did ended up on the outside, the worst punishment a villager can endure. Bitterness at living in a zone so ill-favoured by the weather was one of the most powerful characteristics of the community where I grew up. Resentment towards people born where apple trees blossomed.

This bitterness was a uniting factor without which the two camps of which the village, like all other villages, was composed would have exterminated one another long since.

Anyone who's grown up in a village knows what a Kosovo every village can become, all it takes is dropping a flower petal on someone else's property.

It's thanks to the weather report that feuds don't flare up.

The all embracing, peace-keeping weather.

Madame C has always lived in Finistère.

She was born here, as were her parents and grandparents going back four generations. Her grandfather was a fisherman and drowned off Pointe du Raz, near the site of *Notre-Dame-des-Naufragés*, Our Lady of the Shipwrecked.

Where I lived as a child, there was no sea. Just the snow-covered mountains, and Grandpa died in hospital.

The waters off Pointe du Raz are the most dangerous along the entire coast, the most dangerous in all of Europe. Oil is transported along the sea-routes just off Finistère, one tanker goes down at least every other year.

Not far from here, the *Erika* was wrecked, it happened in the great storm at the end of 1999, the year of the beast, the year before I came.

There are still traces of oil on the beaches; if you walk barefoot the soles of your feet turn black. Birds still die. But the oysters have come to no harm, and the cliffs below my house are covered in perfectly edible mussels and molluscs, according to Madame C.

And all without asking for it; this boundless generosity, this magnanimous Finistère.

The rains in Finistère in the winter of 2000-2001 are unlike anything anyone has ever experienced. The days are made of rain this winter, the houses are made of rain, the gardens, the trees, the waters of the Atlantic turn brackish with all the rain.

Fields lie under water, the damp creeps into the houses. Books and newspapers swell, paper won't fit in the printer.

Morlaix and Quimperlé are the worst affected of the towns I know, towns I have lived in on the way to my Finistère. Wonderful low-lying towns with rivers and Roman viaducts.

In Pont-Aven, the artists' town, sandbags are piled in front of shop windows and doors, everywhere there are barricades and pumps, but to no avail.

My village isn't threatened with flooding, but it's raining into my kitchen and into my neighbour's as well. When rainstorms come in off the sea, I have to bail out my kitchen with a saucepan. I've tried sealing the windows where the rain comes in, but the silicon Monsieur H, the ironmonger, sold me won't stick, the wall's too wet.

I bail out my kitchen and don't complain.

One day during the worst floods I decide it's high time I dealt with my water bill, the gigantic water bill for my first autumn in Finistère.

I drive to Quimperlé looking for the administrative office responsible for water. As ever in Finistère I get sent from one office to another with the kindness and eagerness to help always shown here. I'm wrongly directed, but I am directed. From the tax office where I could pay the bill but don't want to because I'm contesting it, to the local council offices, the social services and the police.

While the water rises in Quimperlé, I get sent round the houses with my water bill.

Eventually I find my way to some flooded barracks with a warning sign saying: *Inondation* — Flooding.

The barracks come under the Ministry of Labour, I'm at the office of environmental health, the water section. While waiting, I read the information sheets on the wall about the quality of water in Finistère — the quality is good.

The water has undergone fifty-four bacteriological analyses, the results of all of which fall within acceptable limits.

The amount of nitrate in tap water varies between 19 and 41 mg/l. Nowhere has the maximum permissible limit of 50 mg/l been exceeded.

The water contains only a trace amount of calcium, and the fluoride content is low. A single little infringement, feeble and of short duration, was recorded in October and related to agricultural pesticides.

Otherwise all is well with the water in Finistère.

There's nothing on the information board about the price being high, and my preposterous water bill turns out to be correct.

I drive back to the tax office, pay the water bill and leave the flooded town, passing water-logged fields.

I drive home and bail out my water-logged kitchen.

It could have been worse, it could have been like it was in Morlaix, it could have been like it was in Quimperlé, poor Quimperlé.

On December 15, the centre of Quimperlé lies under water. The bridges are flooded, the water has risen to the first floors of buildings.

The floods in Quimperlé make the national news.

How high the water has risen is the lead story on the television news night after night.

One evening there's an item about the bookshop in Quimperlé. The manager is pale, he's lost weight. He has a hard enough time getting the bookshop to pay its way without catastrophic floods.

The water rises up the bookshelves.

By cordoned-off areas people stand in silent groups. The sound of water is all that can be heard.

No dogs bark, no children play, there are no cars on the bridges. The shops, the banks, the post office are closed. Water everywhere.

Everyone wants to help, but what can be done?

Helplessly we look at one another by the barricades.

Ministers visit. Jacques Chirac sends his condolences, *le Président de la Republique*.

A state of emergency is declared.

Residents are evacuated by boat.

Night after night images on the news of people in their homes with water up to their waists. Drowned gardens. Furniture up on concrete blocks. Somebody's piano.

Tiles come unstuck from the floor, a person is crying in a ruined kitchen.

Dead swans float through the rooms.

Where children used to play frogs croak.

Fire-fighters, soldiers and civilians keep pumping, but the water still rises.

Fields and meadows are saturated, the earth can't absorb one more drop.

Theories about the origins of the catastrophe are put forward and rejected.

"And behold, I, even I, do bring a flood of waters upon the earth, to destroy all flesh, wherein is the breath of life, from under heaven; and every thing that is in the earth shall die."

Only why Finistère in particular?

"Evil flourishes in damp places" says the epigraph of a novel I'm reading. The book is German. Evil doesn't flourish in Finistère, just frustration.

Finistère is no more to blame for the destruction of the Earth than the rest of the world, and yet it's being punished – why?

There are no answers, no-one knows. The rain rains and the tides take no notice.

My flowerbeds are Mariana trenches, dark abysses. Bulbs can survive anything except protracted wetness, no bulb can have survived this winter's deluge.

I mourn my *Crocus korolkowii*, the poet's narcissi, the precious *Tulipa sprengeri*.

Stonelight

One evening, I steal stones.

It's December. A break in the rain, a rare afternoon, mild and hazily violet.

Winter is mauve in Finistère. The fields are mauve, a violet-coloured winter's what it is, violet against maroon.

You can rest your eyes on this landscape the way roots rest in the ground, the way the earth rests to gather strength for the coming spring.

In the middle of this rainy winter, there's an evening of clear weather. Temporary and fleeting, but a break between showers all the same.

At sunset I go to collect stones, one of the few sunsets in this winter of rain.

The first syllable in most place-names in Finistère is "Plu" or "Plo". I take it for granted that this is the word for "rain", and I don't mind the rain any more than the stones do.

Getting a dictionary of the ancient language that was spoken here is not in my plan. I'm unable to speak enough languages as it is, *merci beaucoup*.

The stones I'm on my way to collect have been deliberately chosen.

The kind of stone I'm out to get this evening is the kind of stone old houses are built of in Finistère. Stone with a velvet surface, ochre-dusted stone in soft shades of grey, from grey to terracotta to a faint dove-blue.

Stones that somehow shine with a soft light. It's the heat in the stone that produces the invisible glow Finistère stone gives off.

On the way to town there's a construction site where somebody's building a house from this very type of stone. There are piles of lovely Finistère stones, most likely counted and numbered by the builder. The idea of stealing the stones founders on the risk of getting caught.

The stones I'm planning to take belong to no-one, nobody owns them. They are stray stones lying about the road, stones no-one will come looking for, stones it's just as well someone took.

All the same I wait until dusk to pick up the stones. Not until the last precious rays of this December sunset do I get going. Even though nobody has been counting these solitary stones, I set off with a feeling of pre-ordained guilt and a couple of black plastic bags in the boot, like an axe-murderer. Nobody will miss the stones, they're nobody's stones that nobody wants.

I still feel guilty.

It's the great guilt from my homeland that pursues me. The guilt exists but not the absolution.

Why one of the most secularised countries on earth should cling so tightly to Christian concepts such as guilt and grace ought to be investigated by somebody who cares. But since no-one does, this is how it will remain. One un-explained fact among many.

You have to live with the guilt and so I do.

Parallel to the highway between my town and the next one, a road runs through villages and past farms where the signposts have cows on them. A narrow road with the steep embankments that border the roads here, one of the marvellous country roads that traverse the landscape in Finistère.

Slowly I drive through the violet twilight, for a while forgetting why I'm here and what I'm about to do. Some deer, in the same predicament, stand like cave paintings against the lilac-brown forest backdrop. When they hear the car, a shudder passes through them and they disappear in slow motion into the mauve dusk.

On the road lies one of the stray stones I've chosen.

I park the car by the roadside. Walk up to the stone. Lift it. Weigh the stone in my hands, feel it. Caress the smooth surface, my Grandma's hands touch this stone in Finistère.

I stand in the violet landscape holding the stone. For a moment I stand there, that grain of sand in eternity, the incredibly slow movement in the stone.

Looking neither backwards nor forwards.

Just being.

The stone, me and Finistère.

The moment is interrupted by the sound of a car coming, getting closer.

The headlights light up the road, there I am in the headlights in the middle of the road with my stone.

Paralysed for a fraction of a second and then I react. Like an animal, instinctively and by reflex, I throw the stone in the ditch, jump into the car and drive off with dirty hands and a car filled with guilt.

The next day it's raining again. I drive over and collect my stone.

Oysters

During the rains L comes to stay for a while. L is a talented young woman who happens to be very beautiful. When she wants to she can be as beautiful as anything, when I met her at the station, it was mostly a huge backpack I met.

L has roots in the same stony soil as me, her mother was a classmate of my sister at the village school.

L used to live in Brittany, in her boyfriend's house, and knows how damp and cold a house can get in winter in this part of the world.

She says my house is a warm house.

Of all the compliments I've received in my life, this is the finest.

I was good-looking for a while too, but it came so late and passed so quickly that it never brought me any joy. The compliments I got I couldn't understand, and the sudden interest my person generated seemed perverse to me. I was ugly after all.

And now L says I've got a warm house and I cherish the compliment, which fills me with pride and self-esteem.

The joys of a warm house are evident only to someone who grew up where winter means month after month of 30° below zero. A warm house is a source of delight and a luxury.

L wants oysters for lunch. Oysters are no luxury in Finistère, they're everyday food like crepes and sausages.

It's raining, we set off to buy the oysters, those distant relatives from a time before man walked upright, this ever-present cannibalism. Wherever you draw the line, something is always killed. Not even the most gentle, considerate environmentalist can avoid drinking water with its billions of living micro-organisms. These limits and their transgressions!

We walk to the harbour. The harbour in my village has the best oysters in the country. Not the biggest but the most tasty ones, the ones with the purest flavour of the sea. When famous people and tourists have oysters at La Coupole in Paris, the oysters come from my harbour or from the harbour near Mademoiselle J's house; Mademoiselle J was brought up on oysters.

She is only a few years younger than L, but L is infinitely older. That's how it is where we come from, you're born old. Nobody dares to be born in winter, spring is too short and summer is too *skälen* (with the stress on the first syllable and a hard "k"), too precious.

Anything lovely and transient was *skälen* to Grandma and her generation. You weren't allowed to use it because then there wouldn't be any more. All Grandma's Sunday aprons, embroidered with hemstitching, her hand-stitched towel-rail covers. The wedding sheets left by Aunt Regina. Why Aunt Regina's wedding never took place I don't know. Because the wedding sheets were too *skälen*, or maybe her fiancé was one of the others, the way it was with Romeo and Juliet.

I don't know what they do with the Sunday-best aprons in Finistère, if they're kept in the cupboards, the huge hand-carved cupboards in Finistère, with fittings made of silver.

L and I know where we come from, and where we're going. We're going to the harbour where they have twelve different kinds of oysters, and a few more.

The man who sells the oysters only has one eye. He's as handsome as a pirate with the dangerous glitter of the sea in his eye.

He recognises me, "*Bonjour Madame*, you're the one who stayed here last summer."

That was me. That is me.

Before I got the keys to my house I rented a cottage in the harbour next to the oyster banks. For a couple of weeks in the summer of 2000 I'd wake up there to the sound of the fog-horn and the tides, the boats floating on the water at high tide and resting on the seabed when the tide was out.

I had my meals on the grass-covered roof. There I sat looking out over the Atlantic, which has no more shore until you reach St Pierre & Miquelon off the coast of North America.

The harbour is one of the many reasons I'll never move away from here. The steep hillsides, the heather in late summer and the forsythia – yellow brightness blossoming like fireworks across the hills in spring. The cliffs. The coastal paths running across the slopes and along the water.

My harbour. What a lovely word. Harbour arbour, such a friendly sound, slightly aspirated.

L asks the oyster man to shuck the oysters. A tin opener won't do according to L. All tin openers are good for is to open a can of fermented Baltic herring. Where we were born you got fermented Baltic herring with your mother's milk, which is why we're so beautiful, the two of us.

The oyster man shucks the oysters on one condition, that we go straight home.

If we want to commit suicide we'll have to do it ourselves, he says and smiles at me just as much as at L, shucking the oysters. With a sure hand, he quickly lays them out in their shells, gleaming mother-of-pearl against the earth-green tones of a glistening tangle of seaweed in a basket.

It turns into a still life, a work from the Golden Age of Dutch painting by one of Vermeer's contemporaries.

When we try to pay for the oysters, he won't let us.

The oysters are a present to L.

"Because she's so lovely," I think, young and lovely, but on reflection I'm convinced I would have been given my oysters on seaweed too. Because I stayed in the cottage by the harbour, because I'm the stranger who has moved to Finistère.

"Thank you," we say.

"How kind of you, thank you for the oysters, *Monsieur L'Huître*."

"It's nothing", "*De rien*," the oyster man says and his eye flashes.

Zen

In one corner of the garden the earth is as hard as granite. All winter long this corner has been under water. Dark surfaces ruffled by storms; a little Black Sea surged here. All the work I put into planting bulbs in October has been for nought. What use was kneeling in my rainsuit trying to decide which end was up and which down of the narcissus bulbs.

Narcissus poeticus.

No *Narcissus poeticus* could have survived all this water. Bulbs rot in the damp, they can survive anything except standing in the wet for long periods. They are called *bulbe* in French, which is the word I misused for lightbulbs in the expensive furnishings shop. These words, how they haunt me.

Winter has destroyed my bulbs and spring brings no hope. Not in this part of the garden. The spring winds arrive and the puddles dry up. The earth becomes rock-hard, cracks form in the crusted soil. This corner has become a stony desert.

It's when I'm about to plant a couple of lilies-of-the-valley that I discover how hard the ground has become. The plants were given to me by Madame C so I can have lilies-of-the-valley in flower on May Day, as the custom is here.

When I try to dig a hole for the lilies-of-the-valley, I can't get the spade in. I bang it like a sledgehammer against the spot where I want to make the hole, but then it breaks in two. The only tool that can get through soil this hard is a crowbar. Hacking out a patch big enough to push down the lilies-of-the-valley takes all my strength and a little bit more, as they will multiply the way lilies-of-the-valley do. There could be twenty lilies-of-the-valley here next year. I bang the crowbar down.

If Madame C were here, I would say "*Voilà*."

In the middle of the rocky desert stand three large stones. The shape of the stones and the way they've been placed indicate that it wasn't nature that put them there. By using the crowbar as a lever I manage to shift the stones towards each other.

Finistère is full of menhirs, upright stones. Scientists have no idea what the stones are meant to signify, apart from the human capacity to move stones. That the stones were raised by human beings is beyond doubt, and that this took place a very long time ago, twenty thousand years ago or more.

It's possible that the cradle of humanity lay in Finistère.

This part of the garden faces the back of the house, since no matter how much there isn't supposed to be a back, the front of the house faces the village road and the back is the part with the garage.

The road comes to an end here, my nearest neighbours use it getting to and from their houses, the farmer drives his tractor over it, and that's it. A couple of hundred metres further on, it turns into a path, one of the wonderful paths that run through the woods and along the coasts of Finistère. At weekends walkers with maps and compasses go by and disappear into the green tunnels of the paths.

Since I'm not just a passing walker but a permanent resident, walking can wait. The path is there, it has been there for hundreds of years, it will continue to be there. The path *is*, whereas my stone garden is in the process of becoming. Instead of breaking up the granite, enriching the hard earth with soil and fertiliser, laying out flowerbeds and preparing the ground for planting, I do the opposite. I bring in more stones and gravel. On a postcard from Japan I've seen a garden made of sand, sand meticulously spread and raked over. A Zen garden not far from Nagasaki, that's the kind of space I'm creating in this corner of my garden.

Monsieur Le R, who despite everything is often in my thoughts, lives not far from Lorient. A town of roughly seventy thousand inhabitants that was razed to the ground in the same war that was brought to an end by the bombs which fell on Hiroshima and Nagasaki.

Lorient is still a high-priority military target.

In the event of a nuclear war, living as close to Lorient as Monsieur Le R does would not be a good idea. In case of a nuclear war today, 10 to 20 kilometres here or there wouldn't matter, not only would Monsieur Le R's department go up in smoke, the whole of Finistère would be annihilated, with globe attached.

Shame on anyone who worries about the future! I'm creating my Zen garden. The peace in a grain of sand is something I'll contemplate every day among my menhirs.

Putting up the bamboo fence to protect the Zen garden

from the glances of passers-by is the hardest thing I've done since arriving in Finistère. When I manage to get one part upright, the other collapses and vice versa. The bamboo fence falls to the ground, it bends in unpredictable directions, it is wild, wilful and wily.

This will never work, I think, but finally, with the help of the thick pieces of twine Monsieur Le R advised me always to have to hand, I manage to get it up. Happily I gaze at my lopsided bamboo fence. I did it.

There are moments when I think about Monsieur Le R, moments but not many of them.

Working alone has only got advantages. There are billions of advantages to cooperation, but right here, right now and in my particular case, there are only advantages to working alone.

Everything can be done. As long as you're left to do it on your own terms, it can be done with a piece of twine or a crowbar. No remarks such as: "Can one really do it like that?" When it's obvious that this is what's being done like that right now. No questions such as: "And how did you plan this? How could you have done it! Didn't you plan the whole thing out before you started moving two-ton rocks?"

No.

I don't plan, it's not in my nature. It's genetic and not a matter for comment. My mother's the same way. Act first, think afterwards, do it on your own, shift stone.

Along the bamboo fence I set out pots made of green-glazed earthenware bought on sale at Point Vert in Concarneau. The fact that the green-glazed pots are chipped makes them look valuable. Precious and old, like objects uncovered in an archaeological excavation. As though they'd been taken from a display case at the art museum in Hanoi where they'd stood alongside celadon jars from 500 BC. In the green-glazed pots I plant sweet peas, white sweet peas. The sweet peas are meant to climb along the bamboo fence and cover it with their fragrant white flowers. Hopefully.

The rock-hard ground is covered in gravel and sand, coarse dark-red street gravel and sea-sand with bits of crushed shell in it. A bucket of sand costs a couple of francs at Big Mat on the road to Brigneau, it takes fourteen buckets.

Some thujas, a ceanothus bush and a laurel tree form a boundary against the rest of the garden. Thujas trimmed into shape by me. I love trimming things into shape, pruning them. A snip of the secateurs and the trunk of the laurel tree has been stripped, the thujas turn into cypresses, the ceanothus takes on the shape of a large mushroom, it looks like the cloud after an atom bomb. I'm pruning my ceanothus bush as a warning to the human race.

With a feeling of great happiness I work on the stone garden. Cutting, digging, gravelling, sanding, sawing and laying stones. Singing. Off-key like my father but with a nice alto voice like my mother.

My father knew the words to the hymns when we went to church for funerals and weddings. He respected other people's beliefs, he didn't sing off-key on purpose. My mother used to part-sing "Oh, Christmas Tree" with Little-

Karin. Big-Karin was Grandma, my large, imposing maternal grandmother, who on the rarest occasions would get her guitar out and sing the song of Little Hans, a long, old and lovely song full of timeless woe.

So This Is What It Means to Be a Human

After a winter like the one we've had in Finistère, it would be absurd to think the ground would ever need watering again.

Had someone told me last winter that I'd have to water the garden every evening, I'd have said that was absurd. But when the spring winds arrive in April it's absurd no longer.

In the daytime, water cannons spread torrents of water onto fields that only recently lay under water, and in the evenings I water my garden.

Of all the things I love here – and that is everything – what I love most is watering the garden at sunset. Watering my plants is all I want to do, and so I do.

It's at sunset that you're supposed to do the watering. Water in sunlight and the roots of the plants get burnt away, so Grandmother taught me. In her manor-house garden the sprinkler system was only on in the evenings, and even then not for long. Like so many wealthy people, Grandmother was very careful with money. Careful to the point of anguish. The capital could never be touched, that hyper-sensitive capital. Nothing was ever said about what would happen if the capital was touched. The capital was tied up and mustn't be released.

Since I've never had any capital, I'm wasteful, and

particularly with water. But, just as Grandmother taught me, I don't do the watering until sunset.

In my garden, the sprinkler system is me. The sprinkler attachment for the watering hose has been broken, so I pinch the end of the hose-pipe between fingers and thumb to make the water spray and then I sprinkle as I please over the entire garden.

I'm an inspired sprinkler. It's all in the hands, the ones I got from Grandma, the best things in life are hands.

These grandmothers, paternal and maternal, and their gifts. No inheritance tax. Grandfather gave his capital away to foundations. A snuff-box was my inheritance. When I tried to sell it, the antique dealer said it was worthless, having a dent in it. Nothing compared to the hands I got from Grandma and Grandmother's advice about how and when to water a garden.

All I want to do is to water, and so I do.

Litre upon litre I let surge through the hose-pipe, drenching the lawn and soaking the roots of the ash tree. Every single blade of grass in the lawn I water, the tiniest clover-leaf, the thinnest stem. The peonies, the roses, the red ones and the white, rambling roses, tea roses, climbing roses like "Madame Alfred Carrière" and the dark red "Senegal" – a climber that thrives in shade and is meant to cover the north-facing wall. "Ingrid Bergman", the modern hybrid, needs water for all of its thirty-five petals to open. I water "Ingrid Bergman" and "Madame Alfred Carrière".

The three magnolia trees, *Magnolia grandiflora*, need a lot of water if the leathery winter leaves are to be shed and the delicate new green ones unfurl.

The *Magnolia stellata*, which flowered on bare branches in the winter, craves water so it can flower again.

All the climbing plants that enclose the garden and the patio, the sweet peas, all the woodland perennials in full shade, dappled shade or full sun. The seeds – sunflowers, nasturtiums, sweet peas, they all need water.

The giant poppies, red and white, the bright blue mountain poppy from the Himalayas, all the poppies whose silken petals the light shines through in June, those poppies as ethereal and ephemeral as butterflies.

You're not allowed to grow opium poppies in Finistère.

Eschscholzia is a poppy that doesn't belong to the poppy family. It doesn't open as freely as a true poppy, holding its petals together until it bursts into warm yellow flowers.

Ever since I saw a bed of *Eschscholzia* last summer I've dreamt of having *Eschscholzias* of my own, but when I tried to get hold of some seeds or plants no-one understood what I was trying to say. When I went back to pick an *Eschscholzia* to show the people in the garden centre, someone had planted potatoes in their place.

Aquilegias, irises and carnations I water. Black aquilegias, a white iris and a dark, dark blue one, scented white carnations. Ceanothus – the shrub with blue flower-brushes and dark green foliage. The pittosporum bush, the thujas, the willows, the four willows of the species *Salix babilonica* "Tortuosa" and a little weeping willow, a *saule pleureur*.

There were already two ancient ash trees on the property, I'm developing ties to these two trees. This risky business of ownership, these dangerous bonds of blood.

You don't own anything, nothing is yours. You water it on its way from seed to dust.

I water the ash trees. Standing beneath the crowns of the trees, letting the water flow down into the roots.

While watering, I pull weeds. Not out of ecological virtuousness. I'm no fanatical ecologist like my father, even though he was right.

There are better ways of getting rid of weeds, ways that are more efficient and more permanent, but permanence is not for me.

It is flow I am after. The pleasure of pulling up weeds by hand, the warm lusty feeling, getting a grip on the dandelion and tightening as it moves, twisting it carefully but firmly, feeling the way the weed releases its hold on the earth and its roots come free.

Rinsing your hands in the water from the hose-pipe, there can be no greater pleasure. The water softly flowing through your fingers. Water as warm and lovely as the earth and as soft.

You can water for an hour and the water still isn't cold.

Rinsing the soil from your hands is a pleasure here, not painful as it was where I grew up. One moment in the water and your hands turned blue and stiff, useless with pain.

The water my father had to use to irrigate his tiny unpolluted vegetables was calcareous and freezing cold. During the winter the pipes froze. Then you had to fetch water from the spring, and nobody who isn't from where I grew up can imagine how cold that water was.

And here I am in Finistère, wasting water.

Of course it's not just to rinse my hands that I waste

water, not just for pleasure or out of necessity. There's an idea behind the watering, the idea of the kind of garden I want.

No plans, no drawings.

No sketch like the one I left behind in the garden at Monsieur Le R's.

My garden is going to be a jungle.

The Zen garden with its sand and menhirs is there for the sake of contrast, the rest is going to be a jungle on my terms. Plants will flourish and climb, lianas leap. Leaves are going to gleam darkly green in shade, colours will complement one another, light will play against darkness.

The image of a jungle is what it's going to be, like the *Douanier* Rousseau's image of the jungle, but an image that is mine.

A real jungle is a mosquito-infested hell with stinking pools and rotting animal carcasses, slimy trunks and black leeches that cling to your legs, your arms, your hands, your throat. Mosquitoes that suck your blood, midges in swarms, clouds of insects making it impossible to see.

You lash out, are struck by panic. It's like on the moors where I grew up, swarms of mosquitoes in your hair, in the parting where your plaits began. In your eyes. Like it was in the jungles of Vietnam where American soldiers went mad with terror.

My jungle will be a calm jungle, safe like the *Douanier* Rousseau's, irrigated and domesticated.

Every evening at sunset I do the watering, it's the best time of the day, when the sun sinks scarlet into the earth, *écarlate*.

Water's expensive in Finistère compared to where I come from, extremely expensive.

If it was just a question of money I might as well be watering with champagne.

The panic I felt when the first water bill arrived wasn't just about the price of water. The panic was about all the unexpected costs, one after the other, together with the exchange rate. Since I arrived a year ago, all the Swedish *krona* has done is fall — you abandon ship, but the ship goes on sinking.

In the spring of 2000, one *franc* was worth 1.26 *krona*, a year later it stood at 1.43. If things keep on like this my Swedish pension — the new National Retirement Pension — won't be enough to keep me in bread and water.

Every evening during watering there's a moment when panic overtakes me and I turn the tap off. I must go indoors and write the book or I won't be able to pay the water bill. If I don't get some work done now, there'll be no more winters in Finistère for me. I want to be a grasshopper, but I've got to be an ant, I've got to start gathering words for winter, or there'll be no more summer to come.

For paradise not to be lost I have to turn my back on it. I've got to go to the computer. Into that gloomy room where the hard disk is murmuring.

I've got to go in, but I'd have to be mad to. I might just as well go crawling back to my homeland on my belly, I might as well be refashioned as a reptile, as a snail, as a trilobite — I'm torn to pieces . . .

So this is what it means to be a human.

I roll up the hose-pipe and go indoors.

But at the threshold I stop and look back, as I do every evening.

I pause and gaze at the ongoing creation.

The drops of water on the petals, the darkly gleaming foliage, the play of shadows, the reflections of light.

Not to take advantage of this moment of evening sunshine would be a blasphemy against the sunset, a crime against everything I've been given. You don't create a paradise to turn your back on it.

I walk back out into the garden, unroll the hose-pipe, open the tap and hear the water flowing again.

Feeling the water pulsing in the pipe, heartbeats travelling into the warm centre of the Earth.

I'm at one with the whole, nothing mystical, just a normal state of being.

That's all there is to it.

No More Waiting for
Monsieur Godot

This thing with the guest room. All winter long I've been waiting for Monsieur Godot to come and start work on the guest room.

To me there is nothing worse than waiting. She who waits does not create, she who waits does not live.

What I've been looking forward to most in Finistère – inviting friends, showing them my Finistère – when will it happen? When will he ever come, my Monsieur Godot?

This endless waiting for men that women of my generation have let themselves be subjected to. Waiting is being passive, a senseless object at the mercy of others instead of a subject acting independently. What might have been possible, what I might have achieved if I'd been spared this insane waiting for men. First for them to come along and then for them to leave.

These, in themselves, totally acceptable men who, by being waited for, take on a significance no human being can cope with without getting nervous.

These poor creatures with their own expectations, their own waiting for whatever it might be.

I thought I'd left the men problem behind me, but since I arrived in Finistère it's taken on an entirely new dimension. In my entire life I've never had so many promises broken. He's coming, he's not coming, he's coming, he's not coming. No plumbing, no lights, no skylight, no tiles.

If someone said to me "We don't have toilets here and there's no electric light," this wouldn't change my love for Finistère one iota. On the contrary, I could face my father and his father with pride, my father the ecologist and Grandfather the elitist.

Grandfather's image of country people was that they all had outdoor privies and used candles instead of electric lights.

But that's not the case here. So-called modern conveniences exist, it's just that I don't know what to do to get them installed.

I'm waiting for Monsieur Godot.

In the midst of all this revolting waiting, a letter arrives from my sister in Sweden. She writes that of all matters reported to the National Board of Consumer Complaints in my homeland, the most frequent are complaints against workmen for negligence and shoddy craftsmanship.

My waiting takes on a brighter aspect.

Since Monsieur Godot has been neither negligent nor sloppy, things can only get better. Just as long as he turns up, and one day he does. There he is knocking on my door, tools in hand. Fresh as a daisy.

I've forgotten what he looks like, but since he begins by laying the pipes this must be Monsieur G, the plumber. He's younger than I remember, while I've aged.

"Mine hair all fall white," I say to Madame C. "What am I to do? Help me."

To which she simply replies, swift as an arrow, that it's not her job to be my *babysitteur*.

"*Babysitteur*," Madame C says, and also that I'm a grown-up person, so my problem with Monsieur G is entirely *my* problem.

Madame C is extremely strict about who a problem belongs to, under whose jurisdiction it falls.

It's the episode involving Monsieur G, the tile-and-plasterboard man, that gets me to change my attitude to all my Messieurs Godot.

Instead of vainly wondering what week, what year, he meant as he disappeared after our first promising meeting with a cheerful "See you at the beginning of the week," I drive to the industrial area where he has his workshop. There I wait until he arrives and then I just pick him like a flower: "In cart, Monsieur Godot, you now."

No problem. He gets in happily if slightly wilted.

He then builds the bathroom walls out of plasterboard, lays the tiles, puts in the glass bricks and does the grouting. In a couple of days the work is finished and the results are brilliant.

Cheek-kissing looms perilously close, we're each as happy as the other.

When I ask Madame C – without in any way begging for help – if she has some kind of theory as to why Monsieur Godot fails to turn up when in fact he does have the time, she replies: "Everybody has time except dead people. It's not a matter of time but of relationships. It takes two to wait, *chère* Madame. The one who waits and the one who fails to turn up. *Évidemment*."

So, finally, I know what I should have known when, at the age of eleven and a half, I started my lifelong waiting for men, and I feel very, very weary.

Sisyphus

The one who never keeps you waiting, the one who never lets you down, is Julien Lepers.

Every evening at 6.20, *Questions pour un champion* is on, the quiz show I watch to broaden my general knowledge and sharpen my linguistic skills, and because of the host, Julien Lepers. *Questions pour un champion* is my college, my linguistic university.

Every evening at 6.20, Julien Lepers comes bounding into the studio to the rapturous applause of the audience. There's no waiting, no picking him up. With a spring in his step, he turns up six evenings a week, fifty weeks a year. The contestants are new every day, three of them will not go on and one will become the champion and get to come back the following day. This makes about twelve hundred a year, twelve hundred contestants and one Julien Lepers.

No-one gets eliminated from *Questions pour un champion* the way they do in more and more of the rubbish programmes on television, in *Questions pour un champion* you just don't advance to the next level.

People don't take part in *Questions pour un champion* for the money, it's about the fun of playing the game, about getting the chance to meet Julien Lepers and talk about yourself, where you live, your job and your hobbies.

All these contestants, all these Michels, Michelles, Pierres, Simones, Luciles, Odiles, Didiers, Davids, all the hobbies that Julien Lepers never mixes up and is so unflaggingly interested in: "Michel, interested in sailing, am I right? Basketball and volleyball? Climbing? Gardening, gymnastics. Scrabble. Horses."

"Your job's doing the book-keeping at a haulage company – how interesting."

"Only nineteen, one of the youngest contestants EVER."

"Any children?"

"Two children – any grandchildren?"

"Say hello to the grandchildren, big kiss."

"What about the wife, a little kiss for your wife. *Un gros bisou* to the children and *un petit coucou* to your husband."

"Is your spouse in the audience, *l'épouse*? What's her name?"

"What's your husband's name? Thank your husband, Odile. With a little kiss."

All these places, coasts, Alps, all these towns the contestants come from, all these villages. Even when there's nothing to be said about the home town of the contestant, absolutely nothing, something must be found. Julien Lepers finds it.

"Isn't that where there's – it is there, isn't it? – that's right, it's in your part of the country, they've got those . . . those . . . those inhabitants . . . Tell us about it."

Only extremely rarely does it become obvious that Julien Lepers is bored, he would be an *Übermensch* if he weren't, which is exactly what he isn't, he's just like us.

Even though we could never do what he does.

One evening the special interest of one of the contestants is determining when Easter should fall in any given year.

"I'm incredibly interested in where Easter ends up," he says.

And Julien Lepers replies without even a hint of sarcasm.

"Aren't we all?"

Valentine's Day, February 14, Julien Lepers asks one of the contestants if she's received a card. She hasn't.

"Neither have I," says Julien Lepers. "Nobody loves me."

They very rarely have single people on *Q*, but Julien Lepers is full of fellow-feeling when they do.

"Still looking? It isn't easy. Single?"

"Me too," says Julien Lepers. "I'm *celibataire*. Totally *celibataire*. No-one will have me."

Our hearts go out to the television set, all the millions of us women, celibate, married, chaste or promiscuous, who watch *Questions pour un champion*.

Now and then the questions are about pop, soul and rock music: "Who is the lead singer in *Zeh Dourres-uh*?"

The contestants are at a loss. The lead singer in The Doors?

Sting? Freddie Mercury? Elton John?

It falls to Julien Lepers to tell them it was *Zhim Meurisson* and then he sings a few notes from "Light My Fire".

Whenever Julien Lepers sings, he nonchalantly blurts out a few notes, just throws them away. Then he stops abruptly.

Julien Lepers is *très cool*.

Miami, the American city, is called *Mi-á-mi*.

The capital of Ireland — *Dewblann*.

This isn't something peculiar to *Questions pour un champion*, Julien Lepers speaks better English than the news reporters on the three major channels. The gene for foreign languages is missing from most French-speaking persons, in its place they have been given the cuisine gene English-speakers lack.

Whenever a contestant manages to get four answers right in a row and the last one right at the very moment the final bell rings, Julien Lepers gets carried away and kisses the contestant on the cheeks as many as five times.

"*Je suis ravi*," says Julien Lepers.

When a contestant gets brain-lock, Julien Lepers is invariably just as consoling.

"What's happening, Frédéric?"

"Wake up, Marianne."

"Leone, you've absolutely got to get your act together. You know you know the answer to this question, it was meant for you."

"Marcelle, why?"

"How're you doing, David?"

"*C'est le cata — c'est le cata — c'est le catastrophe*, Nicole!"

"A black hole, Didier?"

When a contestant fails to make the next round, Julien Lepers is very sympathetic: "It's over, Michel."

"*C'arrête là*," says Julien Lepers, nothing to worry about, it's only a game, and now for the presents.

All those dictionaries and encyclopaedias that are given to the contestants who don't make it to the final, all those *Petit Larousse*, art *Larousse*, poetry *Larousse* and other *Larousses*. Presents, Nicole, presents for everyone, *cadeau*, Didier.

"That's it, thanks for joining us, *cadeau*, Monique."

"We'll let the contestants' smiles say goodbye for us," says Julien Lepers in a black cashmere blazer.

"Good evening and thanks for joining us. *Bon soir à tous.*"

All these *Bonjour*'s, all those *Ça va*'s?

All those *À demain*'s, all the *Bon weekend*'s.

For a year now I've been watching *Questions pour un champion* and Julien Lepers has never worn the same blazer twice. If he has, he's worn it as though it was new.

All those blazers, ties, cufflinks, shirts – all those ties he's knotted and buttons he's buttoned just for us.

There's nothing special about Sisyphus.

You keep on rolling your stone, buttoning your buttons, trying to write your book. It doesn't work, you try again. You start again – it doesn't work. All you can do is begin again, until you realise that that's what it's all about.

At 6.20, day after day, year after year, Julien Lepers arrives to the applause of the studio audience and the expectant viewers in front of their televisions, bounding into the studio with a smile to prove yet again that the Sisyphean task of staying alive is a joy, not a duty.

Cadeau, Julien Lepers.

Nightmares

Last night I could see the entire shape of the book laid out as clear as day. From beginning to end, but when I was awakened by the telephone it was gone.

A journalist wants to interview me in connection with the book, which is in my publisher's catalogue entitled *According to Madame C.*

The journalist takes it for granted that the book has been written.

The book should have been completed, it hasn't been started.

That the book won't be called *According to Madame C* is the only thing that is clear about it.

I'm being asked for an interview about a book that doesn't exist with a title that doesn't work.

The night following the telephone conversation I have a nightmare in which the journalist, in reality a man, is a woman. About my age but older. Dressed in '60s clothes, her hair heavily sprayed, a Kennedy type of woman. Superior and cold. She arrives at my house with a photographer and five chairs in Louis Quinze style. I'm supposed to be photographed sitting on all five. But first my face has to be changed.

The journalist has booked an appointment for me with a

plastic surgeon in Dublin. There's a sign with the word *Morgue* on it.

The journalist issues orders, one is that I have to adjust the air conditioning in the car to the highest setting.

The plastic surgeon can't operate on my face if it's warm.

My face has to be as firm and cold as plastic.

I wake up. There's only one possible way to interpret the dream.

Say no. No interviews. The dream couldn't be clearer: *You know you don't want to. Don't do it. It's wrong.*

Although the dream takes no account of the fact that the book doesn't exist, it's right about my having to say no. The dream has put me in touch with my deepest wish, my No.

My deepest wish doesn't get its way.

I say yes. For the sake of the book. Unless it gets media attention, how will readers find out that it exists?

It doesn't.

I'm in a nightmare and I'm awake.

As far as I know.

I've promised to give an interview about a book that doesn't exist.

Now is the time not to panic, or nothing will get done.

The book does exist.

It's just not written yet.

Narcissus poeticus

One day at the beginning of February – it's still raining, one of those days made of rain – when I least suspect it my *Crocus korolkowii* suddenly bloom in the bed over the septic tank.

All of them have burst into bloom. All at the same time.

Crocus korolkowii comes from Afghanistan. Not that I bought them in Kabul, I bought the crocus bulbs at the airport in Amsterdam together with the tulip bulbs and the poet's narcissi.

I don't know if they still have *Crocus korolkowii* in the market in Kabul, or if they still have a market there.

You don't need to go on an empathy seminar to understand what being a woman in Afghanistan is like, being forced to walk around within a cloth prison, just a little barred window for the eyes in the wall of fabric. Not being allowed to move freely. Not being allowed to talk to whomever you like. Not being allowed to work.

In the middle of March 2001, the Taliban blow up the statues of the Buddha at Bamiyan. Those exceptionally beautiful statues from the fifth century are turned into dust. The pleats of their robes, those wonderful stone pleats, are being turned into clouds of dust as I watch clandestinely filmed video clips on my TV set in Finistère. I see it and read about it in my daily paper. I cut out the pictures of the Buddhas and place them in the folders in which I'm assembling my history of the world.

The blowing up of the Buddha statues doesn't come out of nowhere, the world has been warned. High-ranking envoys have been sent from the West to persuade the Taliban to spare the statues, but the Taliban are merciless. They respect neither the cultural heritage of the world nor women; with the weapons they get from Pakistan they do as they please. Only the rebel leader Massoud and his dwindling band of men put up any resistance. This brave Massoud who will fight to the last drop of his blood against fundamentalism. Massoud even leaves Afghanistan for the first time in his life to travel to the West and appeal for help. The situation is desperate, I read about it in my newspaper, I feel the danger and the losses.

It's impossible to create new Buddha statues at Bamiyan, just as impossible as bringing back the old bridge at Mostar.

Bombed is bombed. You need weapons for that and no-one bids farewell to arms. Without the arms trade, the Taliban would be reduced to using cudgels and catapults made of rubber bands. Without the arms trade, the world would be a better place, but the arms trade is untouchable.

The arms dealers sell their Bofors guns or their warplanes, warships or machine guns. Some arms dealers are heads of state, others are Mafiosi, but no matter who they are – they go free.

At least so far they have . . .

Against all odds my *Crocus korolkowii* are in flower. The cups gleam purple-black against the night-black earth, their brassy yellow insides shining.

They give off a glow, a steady yellow light as though there was a brass lamp inside every crocus; an Aladdin's lamp. Rub the lamp and your wish comes true – my *Crocus korolkowii* have flowered!

So much light against such blackness.

It's beyond belief, but since it has happened, you have to believe it.

Your eyes bear witness.

The crocuses came up and now here they are, like little shining guardsmen.

After a night of pelting rain, a crocus may be laid out flat across the flowerbed, but then the rain stops, and it stands upright again. Knocked flat and out for the count and up it gets again. And again.

No crocus has ever flowered for as long as the *Crocus korolkowii* in my flowerbed in Finistère. Steadfast until the day they stop flowering, long after the hyacinths and the *Magnolia stellata* have stopped.

The crocuses stop flowering, but they will be back. Without my having to visit the airport in Amsterdam.

The crocus bulbs lie in my flowerbed, proliferating.

The same week as the crocuses come into flower, tiny green beaks appear in the bed facing the village road. Fish they are not but my *Tulipa sprengeri*, defying the elements. Out of the thirty bulbs I planted, thirty-three *Tulipa sprengeri* shoot up. Straight stems, red chalices, petals proudly braced in the shelter of sword-like green leaves. Impressive and astounding.

The most surprising tulips to be seen since the tulips that

so surprised the Europeans who visited Sultan Mehmet. Had those already surprised Europeans been able to see my tulips their heads would have rolled right off their necks and down the village road.

A botanical tulip like *Tulipa sprengeri* is by its nature a small tulip. Not so my *Tulipa sprengeri*. They're monumental. Monuments to the fact that they have appeared.

When the neighbours pass my house, they make appreciative remarks about the tulips, but they don't seem greatly surprised. They notice that the tulips have come up, that they're large, lovely red tulips.

Madame C jokes about them, calling them my sea-tulips.

I've no idea whether the creatures called sea-tulips in Swedish are also called sea-tulips here, and I can't find the word in my dictionary. The sea-tulip is a crustacean that lives under rocks; small, hard, sharp, white creatures that have nothing in common with my tulips.

Although I know Madame C doesn't mean to be disparaging, she could at least have shown a bit of good old European surprise.

The tulips go on flowering for months until they finally subside, to burst forth, as forthright as only tulips are, opening their red flowers every year.

As long as they get the care they need, *Tulipa sprengeri* and *Crocus korolkowii* will flower in my garden for as long as I'm alive, and longer.

On one of the first days in May, the Zen garden is nearing completion. I'm totally done in but pleased. Never mind one or two stalks poking up here and there. Like leek-tops, limp, green, unsightly. They disrupt the harmony, but I don't have the energy to pull them up. I'll do it later.

There's no hurry, there's no deadline for a Zen garden, it's not a book.

My body feels as though it has been put through a rock-crusher, like after a night of love making. I sit down in the sand and lean against one of the menhirs and enjoy the fruits of my labours.

Dusk falls. The cuckoo calls, the echo comes back. The rays of the setting sun filter through the bamboo fence covered in white sweet peas.

The lilies-of-the-valley are flowering in the oasis, sea-shells glitter among the grains of sand.

The children fall silent, the dogs are called in, the neighbours close their shutters.

I rest against my menhir.

Time disappears, all is at peace. I'm one with the universe, a grain of sand in all of creation. Grandma is with me, my mother and my little brothers and sisters, my father. All is calm.

I haven't noticed that it's gotten dark.

But it's not dark, it's as bright as day. The garden is lit up as if by a host of white lamps. Vibrating white lightbulbs gleaming in the dark.

The narcissus bulbs, the ones whose tops and bottoms I couldn't distinguish and that I'd completely forgotten, have been transformed underground from the limp green leek-like stalks into pure white *Narcissus poeticus*. Every single

Narcissus poeticus has come up and now they are shining in the darkness of my stone garden.

I planted electric lights, *les bulbes*.

In the scent of lilies-of-the-valley, behind the screen of sweet peas, in the light from *Narcissus poeticus*, I sit while the stars glimmer like chandeliers across the night sky and I am completely enveloped by light.

Even the Stars

Madame C doesn't like the title *The Price of Water in Finistère*. It does nothing for her, she rejects it completely.

The title is devastatingly dry, according to Madame C. There's no pun intended. That's just how she happens to say it.

The Price of Water in Finistère is a terrible title, there's nothing enticing about it, quite the contrary. *The Price of Water in Finistère* sounds like a report put out by a commission of inquiry concerning the declining water quality here. "*The Price of Water in Finistère* sounds like a book about the water problems in Finistère," says Madame C. "It sounds contentious, like a book about a problem. Like a pamphlet. Unromantic and without poetry."

During my first year in Finistère there were a number of demonstrations against the decline in water quality. According to Madame C, demonstrating is one of the fundamental rights and freedoms in a democracy. The slightest infringement of people's right to express concern and dissatisfaction and society becomes a dictatorship. A demonstration against water pollution is quite in order, according to Madame C.

The title of my book, on the contrary, is inappropriate, misleading and ugly.

A book about passion for a place, like the passion I've obviously — *évidemment!* — been stricken with for Finistère has to have a poetic title, something passionate and romantic, a title like *Garden Passion* or *The Stars in Finistère*.

I disagree and tell Madame C that I do.

Poetic book titles are the most revolting things. I know.

"*Dégoûtant*," I say, "*dégueulasse*."

"There's nothing more unpleasant than romantic books by women of my generation who flit round their gardens in cloche hats and flip-flops, trimming their clematises and herbs — *les clématites, les herbes*. Those pestilential phrase-sprinklers, those ladies dripping with *bons mots*. Those . . ." I'm searching for a final annihilating word — "poetesses."

"They should be dusted with *Anti-Limace longue durée*," I say, "sprayed with *Traitement Total, Fungocide, les pesticides*. Eliminated like snails, voles, aphids and other weeds and pests."

"That's how a poet speaks," Madame C exclaims in delight. "You're using poetic licence to emphasise what you feel about those people you refer to as poetesses.

"Because you're a poet, you exaggerate! It's your vocation, you exaggerate and that's *merveilleux*. How you do exaggerate!"

"I do not," I say, which brings us back down to earth.

"*The Price of Water in Finistère*," Madame C says, drily, and far from pleased. "It sounds like an invoice."

"Nevertheless," I say. "*Néanmoins*."

Madame C may be delightful, but she's very stubborn.

Every time she stops by my house on her way to the

baker's or the harbour, she brings up the book title. Tirelessly she exercises her right to protest against it.

She's started buying bread twice a day and no-one could consume that much shellfish without getting ill.

I can't slink past her house without being stopped and having the title of the book brought up for discussion.

The Price of Water in Finistère makes false promises, she repeats over and over again.

According to Madame C, the title first proposed, is much better, according to Madame C, who has no idea that the Madame C the title refers to is her.

I ask her what *According to Madame C* would be in French. And, as ever, she rummages through the various synonyms.

"*Selon Madame C . . . Suivant Madame C . . . D'après Madame C . . .*"

No matter which one you choose it will be more beautiful than *The Price of Water in Finistère*, she insists in that determined way of hers, underscoring her point with a brilliant slash of her diamond ring.

All I can do is agree even though I'm determined the title has to be changed. This is my opinion and I'm not budging.

The reason for the change of title is that there already is a book entitled *Madame* in my publisher's catalogue. Two books with similar titles in the same season and in the same catalogue is one too many, according to me.

Not according to Madame C.

Every book in the whole of world literature could be called *Madame*.

If *According to Madame C* is the right title for my book then it shouldn't be changed. The only thing that should concern me is my book and what's right for it, according to Madame C.

We could discuss the title until the end of our days, but we won't.

One fine day, we realise we will never agree and so we agree to disagree.

"*D'accord!*" says Madame C. "We disagree. *C'est normal.*"

Where I come from there's nothing normal about agreeing to disagree. Nothing could be as abnormal. You have to agree that you agree, or everything collapses.

Being in agreement is more important than blood ties, more important than love and friendship, more important than life and death.

In what used to be my country you have to agree, otherwise who knows what dreadful fate might befall you?

You have to agree or you're considered a malcontent, and being considered a malcontent is something no-one can afford. Being a malcontent means being unemployable. If leaving the country weren't such a Kafkaesque procedure there wouldn't be many so-called ordinary people left.

Madame C and I couldn't agree more that we disagree, that's not the problem. The dizziness that overcomes me has nothing to do with our argument, Madame C has no idea why I'm turning pale.

A vague sense of being unwell that rapidly becomes stronger, a feeling that I might throw up, that I'm going to faint. A tornado is whirling through my solar plexus. All my energy is spent on not exploding all over Finistère. Here I stand beside the existing gate to my existing house with Madame C, the here-and-now existing Madame C, discussing the existing title of a non-existent book.

There is no book with a title to agree or disagree about.

There is no book.

Everything else *is*. The house. The shade-dappled peonies. The bamboo-stalked hollyhocks that grow ten centimetres a day. "Ingrid Bergman", the *Heuchera micranta*.

The wild vine on the party wall, the espaliered clematis, the ivy and the honeysuckle, the potatoes in the potato patch, the nasturtiums on the fencing, the pittosporum by the village road, the purple pansy which survived from seedling to plant and has flowered for four months in a row; everything is alive and growing.

What will happen to the replanted peony remnants remains to be seen, but exist they do, as does the television set. The television and the opportunity it provides to watch news programmes and *Questions pour un champion*. As does the furniture from the expensive furnishings shop and from the flea-markets, the red refrigerator from Conforama, the plates, the bowls and a *faience de Quimper* dish.

Everything exists except the book.

There's nothing as non-existent as this book and me along with it. On my side of reality, there's nothing, nothing is all there is, nothing but absence, but lack. No book, no me.

Madame C can see that something is happening to me, that I'm becoming pale. Convinced that inspiration has struck, she clasps my hands in hers. "*Bon courage* with the writing. Let your creativity loose. *À demain*."

Like a beacon in the darkness her diamond ring scatters reflections as she, more gracefully than ever, gets into her purple Peugeot.

There is no book.

"*Adieu*, Madame C."

"And thus the heart's halves are torn in two," says the daughter of the god Indra in *A Dream Play* by August Strindberg. If Strindberg hadn't written his dream play, there would be no *Dream Play* by August Strindberg, without the writing no drama, no books.

There's a terrible illness that manifests itself in a person's becoming a prisoner of their own body. Bit by bit the muscles lock. When, finally, the disease reaches the lungs and the heart, it's over.

The disease is incurable, you turn to stone and die. Only men are affected by this disease, so my metaphor is rotten. I'm the victim of paradox. On the verge of madness, I stand petrified at the threshold of my house.

I must go in to the computer, the hard disk is humming its song of compulsion, must, must, must.

"You have to pity the human race," the daughter of the gods repeats when confronted with the ways of mankind.

Pity the human race and nothing to be done.

Petrified with panic I hear my pulse thudding in my ears, the hammer beating so hard on the anvil that my skull vibrates.

The panic grows, it fills the entrance to my house, I get nowhere.

There I stand, stuck in the doorway and dying.

I want to write a book about my Finistère, but it can't be done.

When I try to capture it, it becomes words, mere words, and it's unbearable.

I want to put paradise on paper, but when I do, it dies.

Still I want to try, that's part of who I am, without it I'd have no self.

The desire exists, but I can't connect with it.

There's not even a pile of dry pages to burn together with the leaves from the rose hedge, those black-spotted leaves.

"Gather up diseased leaves and burn them," the gardening book says. I burn the gardening book, the sparks rise to the sky and unite with the stars, the marvellous stars in Finistère like rips in the canvas of heaven giving on to eternity.

What I want to convey are the stars themselves, the dusk and the happiness, the gospel to go forth but not the sermon.

I am filled to the brim with happiness, but what good is that?

What I want is to write happiness, not to go around being happy.

The Dump in Quimperlé

When I'm down, I drive to *Éléphant Bleu*.

Éléphant Bleu is a car-wash where you wash the car yourself under a sign showing a blue elephant spraying water over himself with his trunk.

During the period when, every single day, I fail to get started on the book, during the five months that pass from the moment I say to Madame C that one ought to write a book, I frequently visit *Éléphant Bleu*, sometimes several times a day.

I put ten-franc coin after ten-franc coin into the coin slot. I wash and rinse and finish off and then I start all over again.

The foam rises.

When I leave *Éléphant Bleu* in my gleaming car, I always feel a bit better. The sticky layer of despair about the book has been washed away.

For a while.

Somehow it's bound to turn out all right.

Madame C is against all this car-washing. She dismisses the psychological benefit with her slender hands. Psychology isn't Madame C's *cous-cous*.

Madame C thinks I should devote my time to the book.

When I tell her I am devoting myself to the book by

washing the car, she says "*Psschitt*" and makes the gesture Jacques Chirac made on television and which conveys exactly what she means.

"*Psschitt*," says Madame C, belittling my car-washing argument in the same way Chirac dismissed the sum he allegedly embezzled from the tax-payers.

If there was a route to *Éléphant Bleu* that did not go past Madame C's house, I would take it, but there isn't. If I could find a way to tell Madame C that this *Éléphant Bleu* business is my business, not for her to meddle in . . . But I can't.

My inability to simply and straightforwardly speak my mind has not been remedied during my time in Finistère. I am weak and cowardly. Repulsive traits I can't bear and can't put right.

When I'm seized with rage at my incorrigibleness, at my flaws, flaws are all I am, when I'm being driven mad by the world's stupidity, when I've dug all the holes and carried away all the stones, when the car is as clean as it can be, when there's nothing left to do about my rage except become its victim, I drive to the dump in Quimperlé.

I often get offered help with chucking the heaviest things, but since the reason for my being here is to do it myself, I decline in a firm but friendly way.

It's to relieve my rage — congenital, acquired and continually renewed — that I'm here. Just the fact that my rage is continually renewed, that old mistakes get repeated over and over again, is a source of rage. The rage is mine. Nobody but me can do anything about it and nothing makes me as outraged as someone saying I've no need to be so outraged.

Of course I need to be.

I need to be a lot more outraged than I ever have the energy to be and I won't ever be fractionally as outraged as circumstances warrant.

"There's no need for you to be so outraged."

Or: "Why are you so angry?" as the trade minister in my homeland said when I was presented with the opportunity to question his glossy picture of conditions there.

"Why are you so angry with me?"

Why not? I'm no more angry with you than with other Social Democrats who are neither social nor democratic, and who have lost touch with reality — if ever they were in touch with it.

I miss my furious father. There'd be so much for us to agree to disagree about. Or to disagree that we agreed about. But still always disagreeing about what conclusions to draw, what means can be used to achieve one thing or another.

Giving me a subscription to *News from the Soviet Union* when I was boarding with a right-wing hag who wrote columns for the *County Courier* in the '50s . . . damn you, Daddy!

I chuck junk at the dump in Quimperlé. With all the strength I've accumulated in fifty-five years I throw a broken sink to the bottom of the skip. Cracked tiles, cement lumps, a roll of rusting wire fencing, tin buckets, wall-panels, metal bars, a broken radio. A ruined toilet, a cement tub, tiles on top of tiles. Sheet metal against sheet metal.

Throwing away a rusty bathroom cabinet in a rage fails to restore my equilibrium since I've never had any, but it does give me a certain feeling of balance. All the strength I've acquired working in the garden comes to the fore.

I'm tossing bathroom cabinets.

The men who work at the dump nod to each other.

She's tossing bathroom cabinets.

The Freedom of Strangers

Ever since my first days in Finistère, the days I spent with Monsieur Le R, this business of being a stranger has intrigued me.

Since my first days on earth it's bewildered me; in the course of my attempts to get the book started it's been cropping up over and over again. I'm a privileged stranger in Finistère, at best I'm considered bizarre, speaking the way I do and being peculiar, but what would it have been like if I'd come from a country outside the European Community?

I want to hear what Madame C has to say about how usual people like Monsieur Le R are in Finistère.

Many is the time during the past year that I've wanted to drive over to Monsieur Le R's and give him my uncensored views on freedom, equality and fraternity in that well-groomed garden of his, but my not wanting to has been greater than my wanting to.

Instead I intend discussing the subject with Madame C. She knows a child doesn't choose its cradle. You don't have to explain the basics to her.

Madame C is in her garden when I arrive. She's on her knees weeding her aubergines with an appropriate tool for the task and with a cushion appropriate for the task under her knees.

Her sons are resting in the shade of the wonderful lime trees Madame C has in her garden, all three sons. When they catch sight of me they greet me with *"Bonjour Madame"* and wave their cigarettes.

These three sons I've heard so much about, these fairy-tale sons — here they are, all three of them. Two fair and one dark.

The dark one must be the *rappeur* with whose jargon Madame C peppers her speech, he is plucking a stringed instrument. Dressed in a caftan with his hair in plaits like something out of *A Thousand and One Nights*. Black lashes, lilac around his eyes, rather too much, but then I'm not the target audience. A shame, one might say, but a relief in fact.

Madame C catches sight of me, greets me — *"Bonjour"* — pulls off her gardening gloves and holds her hands out to me.

"How fortunate that you should drop by," she says. "We're so seldom all here at the same time, you must have thought I didn't have any sons," she says, with a rippling laugh, and introduces the sons.

Christian, the oldest, works for *Médecins sans Frontières* in Ulan Bator.

"*Madame,*" Christian says, and rises to his feet.

David, the middle son, is a surfer and spends most of his time on some reef in Australia, "*Madame,*" and Benjamin, the youngest, has just got back from a European tour.

"Beaten black and blue by the border police as usual," says Madame C, "perhaps a bit more than usual, a few more slaps than last time."

Benjamin and Madame C smack their palms against each

other's the way young people do in films, a kind of greeting known as *high five*.

Me he greets with a bow, "*Madame,*" and apologises for not being able to get up. The border police hit him on the knees this time, not just on the face and back of the head.

If I were Madame C, I'd be beside myself with rage, completely useless, but Madame C says proudly and matter-of-factly that her son gets beaten up because of the way he looks. And because of the uncompromising character he gets from his father, the passionate man she lived with after her last marriage.

"There's nothing to do but file the usual report with the European Court of Human Rights," says Madame C. "As clear and as factual as possible. It's already been sent, all we have to do now is wait for the acknowledgement of receipt and docket number, and we can file it away under 'European Court of Human Rights'."

At concerts throughout Europe the texts of the complaints are rapped by Benjamin, and on the next CD this one will be included. Madame C and Benjamin slap their palms together in affirmation.

Madame C believes in the European Court of Human Rights the way other people believe in the Immaculate Conception.

She takes my dropping by as a sign that the writing is going well.

"I see you're taking a break." She smiles her knowing smile and puts her index finger with its red-varnished nail over her mouth.

Not even her sons have been told about the book, she

whispers, while revealing in the same breath that Benjamin is very curious to read it.

We then sit together under the lime trees for the entire afternoon, smoking cigarettes, Benjamin plays his instrument and Madame C and the other two sing Celtic folksongs.

Celtic folk music is not my *cous-cous*, but I hum along. The lovely melancholy notes remind me of folksongs from back home and their eternal lament, flowers fading, poor lonely children on their own . . .

A European melancholy overwhelms me, my eyes meet Madame C's. We both have tears in our eyes, large, round tears like crystal balls. She gives me a handkerchief, we blow our noses.

We get up, slap our palms together and say, presciently and simultaneously, "All right."

Under the Ash Tree

It's a blessed morning in June. When the sun and the heat finally arrive after this winter of rain, the garden explodes with foliage.

The sweet peas flower, the jasmine bushes stand like perfumed sentries on either side of the door to the garden shed, whose wall is covered in ivy. When I painted the shed brick-red last summer it was so that the dark green glossiness of the ivy would contrast with the brownish red of the shed and so it does.

Small plants flourish in sun and shade. Plants whose names I don't know because I've forgotten, or because I got them on special offer.

Because I don't want to know. Monsieur Le R used to set out little markers where he had sown his seeds. Tiny little markers on which he wrote the date and the plant name in minuscule letters to remind himself of what he had sown.

I want to forget. That way the surprise will be all the greater. I'm in a state of wonder from morning to night.

Little clusters of black clover that suddenly produce white bells on thin stems. Light green clover with shocking pink bells, cacti with woolly flowers. *Heuchera micranta* "Palace Purple", a dark lilac shade-lover, four plants.

The roses give off their rose scent, the dark red ones and the floribundas, big as cabbage heads. Just as the peonies will give off their scent in summers to come and the peony scent will mingle with that of the roses.

The pergola has become a room with leafy green walls, masses of honeysuckle burst into flower overhead.

The climbing *Cobaea* and lianas of brilliant yellow nasturtiums wind round one another on the trellises.

The clematis casts enormous lilac-blue flowers from narrow tendrils.

When I assembled the pergola at the end of October, the rain was pouring down and kept knocking over the bits of wood I was trying to stand upright or attach horizontally. In my hooded rainsuit and rubber boots, I battled against the storm. I swore and nailed, water running down my back, but the trellis went up.

That this ramshackle frame should now be hidden by flowers and foliage is a wonder. It was the hope that it would be like this that kept me nailing instead of going indoors and lighting a fire.

A miracle.

I ought to be in my study at the computer writing the book, but if I did so on a day like this I'd have to be mad.

If you can't appreciate a day of paradise like this day in Finistère, you've no right to be here.

I have to write the book, but doing it now would be madness. As much time as I have now I've never had, or so it seems; an ocean of time before the book has to go to the printer.

Two months plus four days, that makes sixty-five days.

65 days plus 65 nights.

65 evenings plus 65 mornings.

1,560 hours.

93,600 minutes. If you stretch each minute out to the length a minute has when you're waiting – a minute as long as a year is something everyone has experienced – there are almost a hundred thousand years before the book has to be finished.

All is calm. Bordering on still. There's all the time in the world to get the book written. I can enjoy the sun in my garden until global warming turns the garden into a sun all its own.

The sky is bright blue, a slight breeze in the crowns of the ash trees. The scents of flowers mingle with the faint smoke of burnt laurel and branches.

Everything is in motion and everything is still.

The light flickers as it does in a Monet, this day could've been made by an Impressionist. A day for lying on your back in the grass looking at the many-fingered leaves of the ash tree. Letting your body become one with the ground, feeling the springy lightness of the grass against your back. Putting your ear to the ground and hearing the moles murmuring in their tunnels. Lying still like a spy eavesdropping for information about how to chase them away on their own mole-terms.

It's a day for lying on your back reading a book, it's a day for reading Proust. Letting the long sentences flow in, happily realising that it is possible to write like Marcel Proust. Closing your eyes to slumber in the scent from the jasmine and the roses.

It is a day for dreams, it is a day to take a break.

I lie down under an ash tree with my arms outstretched until the grass grows over me and I am finally at peace.

The War of the Worlds

I want to write a book about my Finistère, but wanting isn't enough.

I want to, but it doesn't, that bloody *it* wrecking everything. Woe is me. Having given my word to Madame C.

Of course I don't want to write the book about Finistère for Madame C, neither for nor to Madame C and absolutely not for myself. Getting things out of your system by writing – what an unpleasant concept. Like going to the lavatory in public. Writing the grief, disappointment, pain out of your system.

A grief that can be written out of your system isn't worthy of the name.

A certain measure of grief must be retained in order to keep one's dignity.

It isn't me or my feelings that are of interest. I'm interested in what is happening, not that it's me it's happening to. Even though the book will be told in the first person "I", it isn't "I" who will be at the centre. Not my "I" and not my body.

This mostly obedient body is uninteresting. So-so. But how practical, such an obvious and useful boundary. This is where it stops, where the skin ends. Beyond that, otherness begins. Outside in that otherness, it's good having your body around you to show that it's a stranger there and as such should be respected.

I need myself as someone to experience events. My self as witness, reliable or not, is what I need myself for. I am here, I observe, I have seen. A self is needed to perceive and experience. The changing of the tides and of the seasons has to be perceived by somebody, like that perennial tree in the forest falling in silence if there's nobody there to hear it.

"It's not the 'I' that is the central character, Madame C. It is Finistère and what happens, it's the events themselves, the changes."

The amazing summer greenery, the rust-coloured autumn, the violet winter in Finistère. The intense mauve of the fields, the tree trunks, my two ash trees. The violet light across the fields between rains. Spring with its faint sepia tones and, once again, the greenery.

What a body can take in through the senses — that's what's interesting. The specific, unique, miraculous world that dies when a person does, the irreplaceable world that then passes away. *Fin des terres. Finis terrae.* End of the worlds.

You don't have to die to kill your world, all you have to do is try to write it down.

I don't want to write a book about the impossibility of writing a book about Finistère any more than I want to write a book about Finistère. Neither about, for, to or from. Finistère itself is what I want to write and that can't be done without annihilating it.

"*Écrire c'est finir*, Madame C. To write is to destroy."

Since I'm now good enough at the language, I manage —

by my standards – to conduct an argument like this with Madame C and she hates it.

There isn't much that makes Madame C furious, but when I stray into philosophy she goes crazy.

"Stop that immediately – *immédiatement!*" she says. "Not one milligram more of metaphysics.

"Write your Finistère, for, or from, to or on, *n'importe quoi*, but do it. Do it however you want, but do it. Please shut up and write."

"Shut up" sounds harsh in translation, but when Madame C says "*Taisez-vous*" it sounds firm but not harsh.

"Write it from the heart like music. Write your happiness, shut up and write."

"Impossible, Madame C."

Happiness has no drama. Without crises, what is written becomes unexciting, uninteresting and unnecessary.

"There are too many books," I say to Madame C.

"No happy books," she answers swift as a swallow.

"That's because it can't be done," I say. "Writing your happiness turns into platitudes. Happiness writes white, Madame C."

"Write it," she says. Curt and hard as a diamond.

At great length and vaguely I try to explain to Madame C why it's impossible.

"You open the door to the garden one morning at dawn. Everything in the garden is covered in dew. The wire fence is shimmering with dew, all the plants, the gate, there are cobwebs between the flower stems, thousands of tiny cobwebs.

"The dew is glittering on the cobwebs, tiny shining bubbles

198

of dew, each and every one as luminous as the others. Everything is white and shimmering. Soft. The garden isn't concealed by the dew, there isn't a transparent veil of dew over it, on the contrary. Everything is accentuated, picked out in shining contours. Distinct but weightless.

"Walking the path down to the bay, seeing the thousands of tiny cobwebs glittering in the hawthorn bushes, is to experience the cobwebs, to be there.

"Writing is tearing the cobwebs to shreds, writing is scrubbing away the shining dew with a horsehair brush.

"A rose fresh as the dew is a rose fresh as the dew and it doesn't look like a rose fresh as the dew. A rose fresh as the dew is not velvet red with a pearl of dew in the centre, a rose fresh as the dew is weird and wonderful. Like a heart laid bare, the white film of the dew strung across the crimson chambers of the rose.

"Simile, Madame C, simile is the death of everything, a rose fresh as the dew is a rose fresh as the dew.

"Everything written is fabricated, wrecked.

"Only what is, is.

"Happiness is itself, Madame C.

"Happiness writes white."

Madame C has had enough now, and she explodes. The diamond ring flashes like a knife, slashing the air like a sword.

"Be quiet now, be quiet. You're driving me crazy, shut up and write. In you go. You've got no time to lose. *Allez!*"

Madame C turns away, opens the car door, pinches her dress together, slides into the driver's seat and snaps on her seatbelt.

Before she slams the car door she says, quietly, but in a tone not to be argued with, "Until tomorrow then."

I can't get a word out, my mouth is as parched as a dried-up well, my lips stick to my teeth, a shudder passes through me.

My whole superfluous body shaking, I watch the purple car disappear towards the bakery. We have disagreed and agreed to do so, but I've never felt such rage in Madame C.

Suspected it but never experienced it.

I'm shaken.

I stagger into the house, up the stairs.

Turn on the computer.

Stare at the screen. The hard disk hums.

The light from the screen oscillates. I stare.

Darkness falls.

A face is reflected in the window, white and flickering.

So many years gathered behind the whiteness, so much experience, feeling and knowledge locked away. The dark well of a mouth, those eye-sockets, the face flickers and disappears.

The moon has risen.

Night has fallen in Finistère. Moonlight. I'm walking in my garden.

I should be sleeping, but how can I sleep?

If I sleep now I might just as well sleep for eternity, the moon lights up the garden, you can see every leaf on the ash trees.

In the moonlight it's as if the scents are visible, drifting faintly.

A streak of silver off the sea glimmers between the trees in the neighbour's cherry orchard, the clusters of fruit shine like ebony.

I follow the silver and walk down to the bay. There I stand on the beach with the Atlantic in front of me, cliffs protecting the bay, tide coming in. Not violently but still as steel beneath the moon.

If this is a dream, I'm the one who is dreaming it, this single self in the great dream; the dream, this solitary self.

Days of Shame

Time passes. A long time or a short time, what do I know? — the skylight brightens and darkens at intervals I can do nothing about.

I disconnect the telephone. I avoid Madame C, I avoid everything and everyone. I don't go to the shops. I don't go out.

The gravity of the situation has caught up with me.

What am I doing?

Who do I think I am?

I can't bear to see my reflection. I close the shutters.

The car stays in the garage, there will be no guest room, no more waiting for Monsieur Godot.

The time of rapture is past, and the time of speaking in tongues.

My skin prickles with shame, thousands of painful pinpricks all over, in my scalp, on my soles, on my eyelids.

For a year now I've been making a fool of myself, an old person playing at being carefree is pathetic and shameful.

Wasting water on plants when most people on Earth don't have decent drinking water.

I know what it's like on this Earth, yet I've been playing like a child in a paddling pool. I've played with reality, made a spectacle of myself and put myself to shame. You can't run away from the gravity of the situation, I ran away.

Grandmother and Grandma – how dare I not respect the dead? Grandma's anxiety, Grandmother's veneration of capital.

My mother's stone wall – why didn't I help her with the stones, those stones so vital in the north against the mountain winds?

Her stone wall is a necessity, mine is make-believe.

My father's political convictions – his utopia fell apart, but he stuck by it all the same.

Grandpa helped build a country in which farmers, farmhands and idiots were valued as much as the rich. Solidarity wasn't just a word for my Grandpa, it was what he did and was. Instead of keeping his dream alive, I've betrayed it, violated it.

I spit like a five-year-old.

All the various ways of looking at life are false, there's only one way, there's no getting away from it.

The dark perspective is right because it's true.

I'm the one who can't bid farewell to arms. Using words for ammunition and language as my weapon, I'm armed to attack what I don't like.

My self-righteousness revolts me, disgracing yourself like this, mercy me.

Being lost for words is how I should be, there are no words for how ridiculous and pointless I am.

There's nothing sacred about my rage, I don't have what it takes to handle it.

Shame fills me. I compare myself to Madame C, her unselfconscious spirit. Her clear-sightedness, no spitting.

When I hear her car stop at the gate, the sound of the engine, I see her before me, how naturally she gets out of the car and looks round the garden, realises I'm not there, assumes that I'm writing. Carefully shutting the car door, she drives off so as not to disturb the creative process.

I have no creative process.

Shame is all I have.

What shall I do now, where could I go?

Far away and all alone, my friends are right. They wanted what was best for me and I let them down.

I let everybody down. Betray and abandon them.

I've played in my little world of roses – now the thorns are being tightened.

The garden – what *use* is it?

My garden is useless, it's futile, it means nothing, a summer pastime and now autumn has come.

The freckles on my hands are getting darker, they're spreading, I can't bear to see them, I unscrew the bulbs.

A harsh light falls from the skylight, from directly overhead. It passes through me like a bolt of lightning, I can feel my heart stop. A malignant tumour in my breast, all will soon be ashes, soon the slugs will take over.

The walls are covered with shells, slimy tracks cross the television set, cobwebs hang in the corners.

Bats silently screaming.

Hope is gone, I'm shut in with the shame. It has caught up with me.

There's nobody home, just shame.

The Transparent Heart

I have learnt nothing, I haven't become a *new* person. There are these days of shame.

Life goes on.

You've got your life, it can't be exchanged.

One day at the end of July – the deadline for the book is August 1 – inspiration arrives.

The lid inside my head is raised, darkness is illuminated, thresholds are lowered. The stress and the tension slacken, the power comes, I have access to my abilities, my knowledge.

I can feel the words come streaming in, from what source I don't know, but the source is overflowing. I'm in that blessed state called flow because the stream of knowledge that has been dammed up suddenly starts to flow free. It runs without my having to do anything, it flows along without effort, continuous.

Clear as spring water.

The book is finished, it is completely ready. It has been flowing in from where it was dammed up and now it is finished.

All that's left is to write it down.

As on a cinema screen, the plot unfolds. The departure, the journey, the search. Setback, crisis, the promise about the book, Monsieur Godot, Monsieur Le R, the moles. As in a Greek drama, the story rolls on towards catharsis.

Content, tone, form – all is revealed.

The book will be told in the first person and present tense.

What happens will happen in the *now* of the book and to fictional characters. Any similarity with living people is unintentional, this is a novel, a prose text with made-up people told in the first-person singular.

Nothing that happens in my story happens in the reality I cherish so much, all of it happens on the pages of the book between the text and the reader, and now I know how it should be.

It's going to be a bright story. But to make the flickering images illuminate the pages, the background must be dark.

The composition must go straight to the heart like music.

It's going to be the story Madame C could never have wished for because the story I'm going to write has never existed before.

One of mankind's many limitations is the inability to wish for the unknown. What a person wishes for must be a negation of what she knows. Like my departure.

I knew where I didn't want to be but not that there was a Finistère, so I couldn't have wished to come here.

The day inspiration arrives is one of the warmest of the summer. The sweet peas have ceased flowering and the sunflowers have taken their place, three metres high, dark red sunflowers.

I have moved into the garden with my papers. Irrelevant papers and journals have been shoved aside.

Everything is laid out on the table in the pergola, notes, rubber, fruit, mineral water, cigarettes. I've had a light lunch and now it's time. The notepad in front of me, the pen in one hand, a robin pecking at a few breadcrumbs on the ground.

Just as my pen is about to meet paper I notice one of the journals. An article about writing a narrative in the first-person singular catches my eye. My eye is caught and stops.

An internationally renowned literary critic is writing about the very thing I'm just about to undertake, I take the coincidence as a good omen and decide to glance through the article.

Which of course I should never have done.

Mankind is a species incapable of improvement with no sense of self-preservation.

I read the article which says that a first-person narrative has to be written in the past tense; a first-person narrative must be told in the past tense to be acceptable.

If the narrator is to be an "I", the story cannot be in the present.

In order for a first-person narrative to be taken seriously it has to *penetrate the deceitfulness of memory, the imperviousness of the human heart, the obscuring distance between then and now.*

Like the hand on a watch that doesn't exist, the pen stops dead in my hand.

"To tell a story is to retell it," I read.

Only when time has passed is narration permissible. Only after the end are you allowed to put pen to paper or hands on the keyboard.

Nothing could be more stupid, more absurd or more idiotic — I have to postpone the story until my love for Finistère is over, I must wait until I'm dead and gone. The story must be told as posthumously as Kafka's books were published.

As the article is written in English, I hope this is a misunderstanding. That there's something profound and essential that I've missed. I take it for granted that the fault is mine because I don't have an academic education. I put the pen down, search for the reading glasses I already have on, and a dictionary. Anything intrusive I screen out — the scent of the honeysuckle, the dark lilac-blue clematis petals that float down from the pergola, the gigantic sunflowers and the robin pecking at the breadcrumbs.

Everything intrusive has to be eliminated; the simultaneous presence of all things must be annihilated. Concentration is selective annihilation, I annihilate myself. I read the article through slowly and thoroughly, eighteen tightly spaced pages that with devastating authority rip my project to shreds.

It says what I thought it said.

The death sentence is pronounced again.

However poorly constructed and obscurely conceived the article may be, with its unflinchingly doctrinaire theses, its authoritarian conclusions, in the conviction of its clichés about the imperviousness of the human heart, it manages to annihilate my inspiration and with it my first-person, present-tense narrative.

A story told in the first-person singular must be played out in the past.

It is inevitable, it says – inevitable. Like a bullet through the heart, a shot in the back, a crucifixion. This *inevitable* is hammered like nails through these hands of mine, these hands I get from my Grandma.

In order for a story to have its place, it must be emptied of feeling, disarmed. Detached.

My story is invalidated, and this is inevitable.

Just as Monsieur Le R discriminates against people in his garden of straight lines, the writer of the article discriminates against stories.

The rage that rises within me is incandescent and glacial.

My fury isn't just to do with the violation I'm subjected to as my story is invalidated, I am furious on behalf of every story under threat.

Every human being is a world that only he or she can describe, and along comes this cultural fundamentalist and says that only one kind is valid. One kind only is allowed to exist, and only in one form.

Stating that only one kind of story can be allowed to exist is a crime as heinous as hatred against a particular ethnic group. It's a crime against humanity.

Not to defend the universe a human being is, is to validate the gulag. The highest form of individualism is the greatest democracy – one for all and all for one. If *one* is not respected, there can be no *all*. That's how it is.

If I let the article go unchallenged, the way I let Monsieur Le R go unchallenged a year ago, I'll be worse than Sultan Mehmet, Berlusconi, Blair and Susan Sontag.

Silence is a crime worse than all other crimes, it is an incitement to crime, it is instigation.

No-one threatened with having their story exterminated or who witnesses someone else's story being threatened should let it happen in silence.

Memory isn't deceitful, memory is the most faithful thing there is, memory is identity. Between then and now there is no obscuring distance.

Then is now.

Now is then.

Whoever doesn't simultaneously live in the now and the then has no roots and no life. And if anything is inevitable it is the transparency of the human heart – how else could the world be seen through it?

This is what I'm thinking as Madame C arrives in her purple Peugeot. Opens the car door, gathers her dress, places her slender feet in their strappy sandals on the ground, opens the gate and greets me: "*Bonjour.*" Then she walks along the stone path to the pergola, as nimbly and gracefully as only Madame C can walk this rickety path, and asks if I've finished the book.

"*C'est fini?*"

"*Madame C,*" I say, "*Célestine, Céleste.*

"The book is not written. Not a word has been set down, not a letter. But rest assured, on the day of the deadline, in seven days' time, Céleste, Célestine, it will exist.

"Not for you, Célestine. Not for me and not for Finistère. For the pleasure of doing it and the necessity. The pleasure and the rage. The rage that makes me the one to write the book and not you, Célestine.

"Stay away and on the seventh day the book will be finished.

"Heaven is my witness, Céleste, the robin and the honeysuckle, the stars of Finistère and the moles in the earth."

Madame C bows her head. As the stem of the sweet pea bends where it meets the flower so her head is bowed. Putting her palms together like a Buddhist, she says with great gravity: "*Bon courage* with the writing."

The diamond ring sends out its light from every one of its fifty-eight facets.

"*Bon courage, chère amie.*"

Her faith that the book will be finished in seven days is boundless, this I know and it is good.

"In seven days then," says Madame C.

"In seven days," I say. Whereupon we kiss one another on both cheeks as though we'd never done anything else, no hesitation as to which cheek comes first.

Madame C hasn't reached her car before the first page is covered.

The ink flows from the fountain pen, my handwriting is open and determined.

The scent of the ink mingles with the perfume of the honeysuckle and the smell from the drains. A flower falls on to the paper, that's part of it.

The gigantic shields of the sunflowers protect me from the world and it from me. The robin skips by my feet and the sun runs its course across the heavens.

The wind dries the ink as I fill the pages from the beginning to the end with a story whose beginning for the moment is:

Far away and all alone

I'm in my garden in Finistère. It's an afternoon at the end of July 2001, a soft haze over the countryside. The Atlantic is breathing tides and seaweed, the reassuring sound of the warning buoy like an owl.

I live in Finistère because